OFFICIAL REPORT

OF THE

THIRTY - SEVENTH INTERNATIONAL

CHRISTIAN ENDEAVOR CONVENTION

Held in Cleveland, Ohio

July 6 - 11, 1939

First Fruits Press
Wilmore, Kentucky
c2015

First Fruits Press

The Academic Open Press of Asbury Theological Seminary

204 N. Lexington Ave., Wilmore, KY 40390

859-858-2236

first.fruits@asburyseminary.edu

asbury.to/firstfruits

MOTHER CLARK

"As the days go by, may all draw closer to our Lord
and nearer to each other."

—*From Mrs. Francis E. Clark's message
to the Cleveland Convention.*

CLEVELAND 1939

Official Report

of the

37th International Convention

of

Christian Endeavor

ະຊ

CLEVELAND, Ohio

Public Auditorium

July 6 11, 1939

Recorded by

CATHERINE MILLER BALM

Edited by

BERT H. DAVIS

Table of Contents

Illustrations

Features

DR. POLING

"Christ calls!' At whatever cost, 'we choose Christ,' and choosing Him, offer our possessions, our talents, our lives, to help make life itself Christlike. Not a new world, but a Christlike world, is the goal of the 57th International Christian Endeavor Convention."
— From the Presidential Address, July 7

LAWRENCE W. BASH
Associate President

Herbert Hoover

International Youth's Distinguished Service
Citation to
Herbert Clark Hoover

HERBERT HOOVER, with an orphan's heritage of hardship, won his way to the Presidency of the United States and to world leadership in humanitarian affairs unsurpassed in the history of his country. More than any other man he represents the unity in successful service of idealism and executive efficiency.

Always he has believed that the highest conservation is not the conservation of forests, rivers, and minerals, but the conservation of humanity: his sympathy has known no race, no creed, no color. His genius as an organizer and administrator has been released for all. We shall not forget that he fed the hungry children of the world and that he continues daily the battle for the safeguards of childhood and opportunity for youth.

It is upon Herbert Hoover, the engineer, the proved executive, the acknowledged statesman, pre-eminent as a humanitarian and friend of youth, that International Youth, through Christian Endeavor with its more than four million members in forty-six nations, confers this award.

Presented by the
International Society of Christian Endeavor
and the World's Christian Endeavor Union
at Cleveland, Ohio, July the sixth
1939

DANIEL A. POLING, President

International Society of Christian Endeavor
Officers

WILLIAM HIRAM FOULKES
Vice President

ARTHUR J. STANLEY
Vice President

HARRY N. HOLMES
Vice President

CARROLL M. WRIGHT
Executive Secretary
and Treasurer

MRS. HELEN LYON JONES
Vice President

STANLEY B. VANDERSALL
Associate Secretary

PAUL C. BROWN
Extension Secretary

ERNEST S. MARKS
Field Secretary

10

HEADQUARTERS
World's Christian Endeavor Building, 41 Mount Vernon Street, Boston, Massachusetts

Awards and Recognitions

REGISTRATION CONTEST

Numbered Banners

No. 1 District of Columbia

No. 2 West Virginia

No. 3 Utah

No. 4 Delaware

No. 5 Pennsylvania

Next five to Golden Rule Union, Wisconsin, Tennessee, California, New Hampshire.

Parade Positions

First Place—District of Columbia

Second Place—West Virginia

Third Place—Utah

Fourth Place—Delaware

Fifth Place—Pennsylvania

Program Committee

Dr. J. Gordon Howard, *chairman*	Frederick L. Mintel
Rev. Leslie G. Deinstadt	Dr. Daniel A. Poling
Harry N. Holmes	Fred W. Ramsey
Mrs. Helen Lyon Jones	Rev. Arthur J. Stanley
Norman Klauder	Dr. Harry Thomas Stock
Miss Sarah E. McCullagh	Dr. Raymond M. Veh

Dr. Stanley B. Vandersall, *secretary*

I

Cleveland — Again!

IT is a Christian Endeavor axiom that an International Convention held in Cleveland is bound to be a convention of exceptional inspiration and power. Veteran Endeavorers still talk of the glories of "Cleveland '94." Thousands remember vividly the joy and challenge of "Cleveland '27," and the great host of keen, enthusiastic young people who are the Christian Endeavor leaders of today are unalterably convinced that no convention will ever surpass "Cleveland '39"!

It was a glorious convention!

Inevitable that it should have been. The convention theme, CHRIST CALLS, met instant response in the heart of youth. The development of that theme in tremendous meetings of inspiration and challenge, in thoughtful group conferences, in quietly beautiful experiences of worship was carefully planned and skillfully carried out.

Many people dreamed and prayed and worked to produce the most significant program any Christian Endeavor convention has ever offered. Dr. Poling and the officers of the International Society of Christian Endeavor gave it earnest and untiring consideration. Dr. J. Gordon Howard, Director of Young People's Work for the United Brethren Church, worked tirelessly with a large and representative committee to perfect every detail of the program.

No easy task, that of a program committee! To determine program content—addresses to be made at general sessions, subjects to be considered in the educational conferences, adequate opportunity for worship, sufficient chance for fellowship in recreation, time for denominational rallies and state meetings and, somehow, a little time left for sleep! To find the very best speakers, to choose the most capable conference leaders, well-informed in their particular branch of religious education and skillful in directing discussion, to appoint conference chairmen—the task of a program committee is a long and tedious one.

Because that task was well done, Cleveland Convention delegates not only had their spirits "stabbed broad awake"—they also had direction given to those awakened spirits. They learned new ways of Christian Endeavor service in a troubled world. They shared experiences and encouraged one another. They could confidently expect the results of the convention to include new determination to find the Christian solution of present-day problems. They will seek a clearer idea of the entire scope of Christian Endeavor, better leadership in Christian Endeavor societies and unions, deeper consecration to the work of Christ and the church.

It was a glorious convention!

TWO GREAT CHAIRMEN

FRED W. RAMSEY
Cleveland Committee

J. GORDON HOWARD
Program Committee

Inevitable that it should have been—with a local convention committee headed by Fred W. Ramsey and Fred L. Ball, whose efficient leadership was proved in the 1927 convention. The convention committee spared no effort in preparing for the comfort and delight of the delegates. All Cleveland conspired to make the delegates feel at home. Where, indeed, could they feel more at home than in this beautiful city which has always been a center of Christian Endeavor?

Cleveland's places of business welcomed the convention as heartily as did its many churches. The police were alert to direct delegates and to give them the feeling of honored visitors. Cleveland's gracious mayor was a most cordial host. Even Lake Erie put on its best blue sparkle and waved a greeting to the delegates, while the weather demonstrated a wide range of Cleveland temperature.

It was a glorious convention!

Inevitable that it should have been—with friendliness its keynote. Every delegate commented on the joy of fellowship with so many people, from so many varied and interesting places. Many denominations were represented, but all who came were concerned with a common purpose. Members of different races shared experiences of friendship with no dividing race consciousness.

The Delegates Said

Especially commended in the reports turned in by state delegations, at the close of the convention, were the following features:

The Quiet Hour sessions; Fellowship of Prayer; conferences on Christian Endeavor's part in the total program of the church; conferences on union work, as conducted by Ernest S. Marks; addresses of Dr. Poling. Dr. Evans, and Dr. Judd. in particular; inter-racial mingling with no apparent consciousness of race; the Lord's Supper; the friendliness and fellowship found everywhere among the delegates; the convention banquet; many features of the parade. including the large number of marchers and the attention given to starting on time; clear expression of the new program of "Christ Calls!" to he found throughout the conference sessions. youth addresses, and other addresses.

Of Human Interest

A youth convention like this becomes within a few hours a sort of community, in which events serious, significant, memorable, and also humorous occur, hour by hour. News hunters among the convention staff and the sharp-eyed reporters of the convention city's daily papers never quite catch up with the daily happenings among the convention delegations. Only in the days and weeks that follow adjournment does the story come into a form which compels the thought—"How interesting, or worth while, or mirthful, this or that would have been, had the convention itself known about it through a statement from the platform or a paragraph in the newspaper!"

Since the last session adjourned, one state delegation has reported such incidents as these:

A group of six rode thirty-three miles around Cleveland looking for the church at which a well-beloved field secretary was scheduled to speak. The patient travelers never found this church.

A girl brushed her teeth with white shoe polish, in her haste to catch up with other convention-goers who had risen earlier.

"They said it was the management. but maybe it wasn't." At any rate someone called several rooms. full of delegates from one state. at 1:30 in the morning, to say that the rooms would have to he vacated so that painters could get at their work later that morning.

An eastern state union's delegates will remind its field secretary for many a year of the extensive quantity of lemons he sucked in an effort to avoid seasickness, while traveling to Cleveland on a Great Lakes boat.

Clad for the parade, a Wisconsin "dairy girl" stopped in at a Cleveland bank to cash a check. The policeman on duty warned her not to attempt to "sell anything" without a city permit.

A typical convention audience in one of the stirring sessions in Cleveland's Public Auditorium.

II

Christian Youth in Convention Assembled

FOR long months thoughts of youth turned toward Cleveland. Now at last the time of waiting was over! From every part of the continent, young men and women rushed into the convention city, where the red-and-white emblems of Christian Endeavor everywhere emphasized the welcome of Cleveland's hospitable citizens.

Delegates came in great crowds (Pennsylvania sent more than 400) in special trains and busses. They came in small groups—in expensive new automobiles and battered old jaloppies. Privileged individuals traveled by airplane; less privileged individuals hitch-hiked. Albert Windle, a seventeen-year-old student at Temple University, Philadelphia, who is blind and partly deaf, was the first delegate to arrive. He hitch-hiked from Coatesville, Pa., in nineteen hours. A Kentucky mountain delegation of eleven came with their pastor in a station wagon, cooking their food (brought from home) over roadside camp-fires. It matters not at all how you travel to convention—what matters is that you do arrive!

Incredible to think, on Thursday morning, that hundreds of additional delegates, unable to obtain a week-long vacation, would arrive for the week end. For on Thursday morning it seemed as if all the young people of America had come to Cleveland! Frank Stewart, church editor of *The Cleveland Press*, wrote, "Singing and cheering youths from 48 states today pinned the badge of Christian Endeavor on the lapel of Moses Cleaveland."

"Hawaii is here, too," smiled James Misajon and his lei-decked fellow delegates.

"*We* make this an international convention," explained the charming young people from Canada.

To most of the delegates a convention was a new experience, but some young people had attended several international conventions.

"Your first one is always the most exciting," they admitted, "but you'll want to go on to the next one and it will be thrilling, too. We expect to have a wonderful time in Cleveland!"

Miss Clara Dohme of Maryland, arriving with her precious collection of convention badges arranged on a square of black velvet, had attended her first International Christian Endeavor Convention in Cleveland in 1894, has missed only four since that time, and has attended seven World Conventions also. She found them all thrilling!

Honeymooners Among Us

At least two couples came to convention on their honeymoons. Mr. and Mrs. John Thompson came from Pittsburgh. Leslie G. Deinstadt, field secretary for Massachusetts, brought his bride, the former Evelyn Fox of Wisconsin, where she was the state union president.

Miss Edith Clark of England and a group from Australia represented the British Empire and were most welcome and honored delegates.

Five hotels, the Y.M.C.A., the Y.W.C.A., and countless private houses were the Cleveland homes for the delegates. But no sooner were their suitcases unpacked, their neckties straightened, and their curls brushed, than the delegates were out of their rooms, impatient to explore all of Cleveland, especially eager to see the Convention Auditorium.

"Let's go see it right away!" urged the pretty girl from Kansas.

"I *can't wait* for the convention to begin," confessed the tanned young man from New York.

Heard Among the Throngs

Nobody (except serious members of the Board of Trustees, mopping their brows and thoughtfully considering Christian Endeavor programs and policies in their meeting room at the Hotel Statler)— *nobody* could sit still, for there were so many things to see and so many new people to meet. And so much to say.

"I'm glad Pennsylvania had a lot of registrations. Our delegation is to sit at the very front of the Auditorium. Imagine getting a real close-up of Herbert Hoover! Did you ever read about what he did in Belgium—and in China?"

"Here comes the Golden Rule Union's delegation! Look at those gorgeous costumes!"

"That's Arthur Stanley, the Associate President. He represented Christian Endeavor at the Oxford Conference. Do you know who will be sent to the World Christian Youth Conference at Amsterdam?"

"The banquet will be Monday night. Let's get our tickets now, before we spend too much money on other things."

"Will there be a recreation demonstration? I must make a note of the time."

"Be sure to come early to Quiet Hour service. You won't want to miss a minute of it."

"It's time now for our pre-convention prayer meeting. Jim, let's go in." (They started their convention experience with prayer.)

Service of Prayer for the Convention

Not all the delegates who were in Cleveland came to the Thursday

Dr. Poling with Ernest Richardson, Waco, Texas, and Miss Genevieve E. Park, Lincoln, Nebraska, winners of the contest conducted by "The Lookout."

afternoon service of prayer for the convention. Many were still busy finding their Cleveland homes and getting settled. Those who did come promptly and quietly to Room A in the Music Hall found the service one of unusual enrichment. All the plans for the convention were made now; Christian Endeavorers had done their best to prepare for a glorious experience. The results were in God's hands. Very reverently the Endeavorers in Room A sought His blessing upon the convention, on speakers and leaders and delegates.

"Dad" Reiner, Christian Endeavor's beloved leader from Chicago, Dr. W. E. Peffley, and the Rev. Elmer Becker guided the meditation and prayers of the group, speaking of the great need of prayer and of its tremendous power. Many delegates participated in brief and ardent sentence prayers. Thoughtfully sung prayer hymns expressed the feelings of all the delegates.

At the end of this brief service, which for so many young people was a blessed beginning of a wonderful experience, Dr. Reiner said: "God hears and knows our needs. Many things have been wrought by prayer. Who knows what great things may come to pass through this gathering this afternoon?"

Great things *did* happen in the convention, which formally began a few hours later. Who can minimize the place of this sincere prayer service in helping to make them possible?

A part of the convention banquet on Monday evening. (See also page 30)

III

A Glorious Opening Session

LONG before the appointed hour the brilliant lights of the Convention Auditorium shone on a sea of color as state and provincial delegations found their places. The air tingled with anticipation while thousands of Endeavorers listened appreciatively to a pleasing organ recital and gazed eagerly at the huge, fern-bordered stage.

Suddenly the stage was filled with people. Rising tier upon tier at the back were the youthful members of a large chorus, with their leader, Earl Evans, before them. There were Harry F. Fussner and A. J. Seith at the two grand pianos. There, as beaming and eager as if this were his first convention, was Homer Rodeheaver (with his trombone, of course!) presenting Mr. Evans to the convention.

"All Hail the Power of Jesus' Name!" the pianos began and with "Rody" leading, the convention burst forth into joyous song. "All Hail, Emmanuel," sang the convention chorus. "We Choose Christ," theme song of the Philadelphia Convention, followed: then "Lead Me to Calvary," the second stanza of which was carried by the trombone. with delighted Endeavorers humming an accompaniment. "He Lives!" was sung in tones of triumph. A few moments later the convention rose as one person as the President, Dr. Daniel A. Poling, and Mrs. Poling, and the officers of the International Society of Christian Endeavor came upon the stage.

"I declare the 37th International Christian Endeavor Convention in session!" said the President, in clear and ringing tones.

Miss Blanche Yeomans, of Kansas. led the worship service on the theme, "Christ's Call to Today's Youth," and the delegates reverently followed.

The addresses of welcome were unusually gracious and interesting. The Rev. Thomas D. Ewing spoke on behalf of the Cleveland Church Federation. Said Mr. Ewing:

"Mayor Burton will tell of Cleveland's variety of national groups. of her pride in a rich heritage from Europe and in her strong churches in which are represented every nation and many races. I want to say to you that the task of the churches is to unite the Christian people of all denominational. national and cultural groups—to unite them all in allegiance to Christ.

"The Cleveland Church Federation through its standing committees' activities and through cooperation in movements like the National Preaching Mission forgets that which divides. The things in which we agree are so much more important than the things in which we disagree! The churches of Cleveland are united for Christ! The churches of Cleveland welcome you! No united movement is greater than Christian Endeavor."

Hon. Harold H. Burton, mayor of Cleveland, was good-looking and gracious. With his charming wife he appeared several times during the convention.

"Cleveland expects this Christian Endeavor Convention to give it new inspiration and to strengthen its confidence in the future," Mayor Burton declared. "To know Cleveland you must know where it came from. Connecticut was first a royal grant from the king of England—a grant of land the width of Connecticut from the Atlantic Ocean to the South Seas! Pennsylvania and New York took shares of this grant and a strip of land 120 miles west of the Pennsylvania line was reserved by Connecticut.

"Cleveland, first called New Connecticut, was founded by General Moses Cleaveland, who hoped that the town would some day grow as large as New Windham, Connecticut! Sixty-five per cent of Cleveland's people are foreign born or have foreign-born parents. Twenty-five nationalities are represented in Cleveland's population. Cleveland clings to her early ideals and adds the gifts of other nations. In the American Peace Gardens you will find a garden representing each nation, in each a monument to the cultural leaders of that national group. During a recent convention earth from Germany and allied nations was placed in the garden. It was a Slovenian-American, Louis Adamic, who said, 'America is not so much a place as a people.'

"Young people, America will be what you make it. I welcome you as an inspiration to Cleveland, and call to your attention the statue of Tom Johnson in the Public Square. You will read upon it this verse:

> " 'This man forsook the few to serve the mass,
> He found us leaderless, groping, blind,
> He left the city with a civic mind,
> And ever, with his eyes upon the goal,
> He left the city with a civic soul.' "

Introducing Fred W. Ramsey, chairman of the Cleveland convention committee, Dr. Poling said:

"Fred W. Ramsey, convention chairman, succeeded John R. Mott in the leadership of the Y.M.C.A., and is known everywhere for his loyalty to Christ and the church. I present Mr. Ramsey, sacrificial chairman, to bring his address of welcome."

Mr. Ramsey, Commissioner of Welfare for the City of Cleveland, responded.

A prayer for the convention was then made, an offering given, and a beautiful selection sung by the chorus. The entire convention sang "Onward, Christian Soldiers."

Mr. Hoover Arrives

Once he had spoken to an International Christian Endeavor Convention—San Francisco 1931—from his desk in the White House in Washington, and thousands of young people had stood listening tensely to his broadcast message. Once the Christian Endeavor Field Secretaries' Union had been received by him at the White House. Always he has

President Poling and Mr. Hoover
Dr. Poling holds the citation presented to the convention's distinguished guest.

been a hero to Christian Endeavorers, whatever their political preferences. For this man, who became President of the United States after a heroic career of saving countless lives in Belgium and of adventure in China, had been a Junior years before in an Oregon Christian Endeavor society.

Very quietly he came out upon the stage, and the convention stood to honor him—stood singing, "My Country, 'Tis of Thee," and welcoming with smiles the Hon. Herbert C. Hoover. Delightfully, Mr. Hoover smiled back. He continued to smile as the business of the convention was carried on until the time of his own address, which was to be heard not only by the convention but by radio audiences all over the continent.

Dr. Stanley B. Vandersall, Associate Secretary of the International Society of Christian Endeavor, spoke briefly on "Our Work as an Interdenominational Movement." He presented to Dr. Poling and the convention the following denominational leaders of young people's work:

Miss Lucy M. Eldredge—Congregational-Christian Church
Mr. Moses M. Shaw—United Presbyterian Church
Mr. J. W. Eichelberger, Jr.—African Methodist Episcopal Zion Church
Dr. J. Arthur Heck—Evangelical Church
Rev. Elmer Becker—Church of the United Brethren in Christ (old Constitution)
Rev. George Oliver Taylor—Disciples of Christ
Rev. Herbert L. Minard—Editor of *Front Rank*
Dr. Raymond Veh—Editor of *The Evangelical Crusader*
Dr. Manson Doyle—United Church of Canada
Mrs. Mary Jordan Sweet—Society of Friends
Dr. J. Gordon Howard—Church of the United Brethren in Christ.

Carroll M. Wright, Financial Secretary and Treasurer of the International Society, then spoke on "Our Work as an Organization," and presented the Christian Endeavor Field Secretaries, Regional Vice Presidents, and Departmental Superintendents. Like the denominational leaders, these faithful, consecrated young men and young women were given enthusiastic applause.

Then—exactly at 9:30—the convention was "on the air" and the memorable Service of Recognition for the Honorable Herbert Clark Hoover began. Dr. Poling and Mr. Hoover moved toward the microphone, and the convention and the radio audience listened to Dr. Poling's presentation* and Mr. Hoover's thought-provoking address. Small wonder that after that address the delegates went very quietly to State Quiet Hour meetings and prayed for strength to follow the course of action to which Mr. Hoover had challenged them.

A New Proposal for American Action

Address by

Hon. HERBERT CLARK HOOVER

Last night I spoke on the *American Magazine* hour against sending our youth to war in foreign countries again. I stated, however, that America can be of service to peace and humanity. Among other things I suggested that we can build up the standards of decency in the world. We can take action which will lessen both the causes and the barbarities of war. We can do it without involving ourselves in foreign wars. I shall make a concrete proposal for such constructive action tonight.

You represent the youth of many nations. And you are profoundly interested in peace. You are profoundly interested in the growth of humane spirit in this world. And if war should come you are interested in all possible protection of humanity in that war.

Last night I referred to the suffering of women and children in the Great War. I know. For years it was my sole occupation to care for tbe homeless, the

---

* The official text of the award of recognition made to Herbert Clark Hoover appears in the opening pages of this volume.

foodless, the frightened, and the helpless. I have witnessed their sufferings in twenty nations. And when one speaks to me of war, I do not see the glorious parade of troops marching to the tunes of gay music. I do not think of great statesmen planning and worrying in their chancellories. Nor do I think of those dazzling chambers where the peacemakers of the world meet to settle the affairs of mankind. I see the faces of hungry, despaired, and terrorized women and children. These are the real victims of modern war.

The violence of war is year by year falling more and more horribly upon the civilian populations. Starvation by blockade and killing from the air have become weapons of attack in modern war. At least they have become methods of reprisals. Put bluntly, that means wholesale killing of women and children

The Food Blockade

Industrial civilization has increased the numbers of people in many countries far beyond their domestic food supplies. They must import food from overseas

In the last war both sides struggled to bring victory by starvation of the whole enemy people. The food blockade by the Allied Governments on one side and the ruthless submarine warfare by the Central Powers on the other had starvation as a purpose. In the last war both sides professed that it was not their purpose to starve women and children.

But it is only hypocrisy to say that the blockade is directed to starvation of soldiers, munition workers, or government officials. They levy a first call on all food. It is only the deluded who think that these ever starve. Armies and munition workers were not short of food in blockaded Germany in the last war All over Europe it was the women and children who, weakened from scanty food supplies, died not in hundreds of thousands but in millions It was the children who grew up stunted in mind and body. Who can say that the confusion in Europe today is not partly the result of the horrible lives of the children of those years?

Death from the Air

And in equally dreadful sense I saw a newer method of war develop The bombing of civilian populations from the air first appeared as a part of war strategy during the Great War. The bombing plane was then scarcely developed It was a weakling when the Germans used it against British and French cities But even then I have seen with my own eyes a score of air raids where terrorized women and children flocked to cellars uselessly and frantically to escape a rain of explosives.

No country then possessed great numbers of these planes built purposely for bombing. Today each nation numbers its fleet in thousands And today each plane will carry ten times the death-dealing explosives In terror every European nation is equipping everybody, even the babies, with gas masks. Every country is preparing to evacuate women and children from the cities One of the dreads of Europe today is that these great fleets of planes will be used to destroy whole cities.

Again it is hypocrisy to say that the sole purpose of bombing planes is to destroy soldiers, communications, and munition works. That is not the full intention The purpose is terror and weakening of the morale of the civil population. That means the killing of women, children. The experience in China and Spain in the last two years only confirms our worst fears

The Strategy of Modern War

The ancient chivalry for the protection of women and children has departed in the violence of the times. But why these pressures and terrors against women and children?

To break down the morale and resistance of the civil population at home has become a part of the methods of war. There was a time when wars were carried on exclusively by soldiers and sailors. The civil populations went about their routine daily tasks.

Today war is a battle of whole peoples. They must be mobilized to the last atom of their economic and emotional strength. All fit young men and boys are conscripted and thrust into the battlefields. The pressure on their women and children by the enemy is supposed to react upon the conscripts at the front. It is supposed to weaken their courage and the resolution of these huge armies. Or it is presumed to make the enemy people supplicate its own government for peace.

The Menace of Increasing Armament

Whether the intention is deliberate, direct attack, or only a threat of reprisals, this fear for their women and children is one of the driving forces of increased armament by every nation

One impelling reason for increasing naval fleets given by every country in Europe and Asia is not only to blockade the enemy's food but to keep open the lanes of their own food supplies. Up to the last war the strength in the starvation battle rested with the country which possessed the battleships. But during that war the German submarines demonstrated a capacity to destroy the food supplies destined to England and France, even against their superior fleets. It brought British and French food supplies into extreme jeopardy. Since then the submarine has been greatly improved and its numbers have been vastly increased.

One of the impelling reasons for unceasing building of bombing planes is to prepare reprisals for blockade starving of women and children or reprisals for air attacks

This killing of women and children haunts every move of power politics. It drives not alone to armaments It drives to more and more military alliances that breed war.

Until this menace of killing women and children by food blockade and from the air is removed, there will be little relief from increasing navies and air fleets There will be little decrease in the fear that is driving the world to its own destruction

The standard of living, the comfort of all men, is today being steadily lowered by this race of armaments It is the backs of the men and women who toil that carry this load of war preparedness during peace. It is nonsense to say this is paid for by the rich. The pay comes from the productivity of the people. It is breaking the backs of nations today.

And the United States builds correspondingly to meet the menace of these swelling navies and air fleets.

Objections to Limitation of War Methods

Surely the time has come when men should renounce the starvation and massacre of women and children as methods of war.

I am well aware that any protest or any proposal to limit these horrors in future wars will be decried by the militarists as futile. They will say that the world has tried to do this sort of thing and failed. Civilian authorities in these desperate times may decry it as impractical. It will be said that war is itself immoral and to suggest moral restraint in conducting war is a hopeless contradiction.

Even if nations subscribe to it in peace it will be said there can be no dependable enforcement after war begins. Long reasons will be adduced to support its unenforceability. It will be said that in modern war national existence is at stake. National institutions will be destroyed by the inevitable revolutions that follow to the defeated country. Long years of indemnities and oppression are the penalty of defeat to the vanquished. Therefore, it will be said that despite any agreement to protect women and children, every nation when once engaged in war will justify every weapon as a part of its defense, no matter what their humanitarian agreements may be. I shall comment upon some teeth that could be put into enforcement in a moment.

Fallacies Often Revived

The old fallacy will be produced that the prospect of war becoming more terrible frightens nations into keeping the peace. But the fact is nations go to war out of desperation at these very threats. The fear of frightfulness does not make for peace. It creates fear, hate and desperation which drive nations to war. The prospect of killing of women and children makes war more likely

Another old fallacy will be produced That is, the more terrible war is, the quicker the sickened nations will make peace. But war has become more terrible every year since the invention of gunpowder. Every half century has seen more and more men sacrificed on the battlefield. It has seen more and more women and children sacrificed at home. Human courage rises far above any terror yet invented.

This same fallacy pretends that putting the screws on the civil population gets war over quicker. Such a policy is thus said to be more humane The last war proved that starvation and bombing only sharpened hate and hardened resolution to continue.

Even supposing all these arguments are true, are we to accept defeat of international decency? Are we not to try every method, explore every channel, that might allay these causes of war and armament and that might lead to protection of the lives and minds of innocent women and children? Must we accept such a collapse of Western civilization? Must we accept the despair of return to barbarism?

A Proposal

I am going to risk a proposal that might end the worst of it

My proposal is that all nations that are willing to do so should enter an agreement—

1. *That vessels laden solely with food supplies should be placed upon the same basis of immunity as hospital ships. They should go freely. Blockade should not apply to them. There should be no attack upon their passage by either warships or submarines.*

2. *That there shall be no bombing of civil populations and no bombing anywhere except in the field of actual fighting men on land or sea, and at works devoted strictly to munitions.*

Nations that are not willing to enter such obligation will have at least declared their shameful devotion to barbarism. They will be proved outcasts from civilization.

There is humanity in the peoples of all combatant nationalities. Their own public opinion is shocked by barbarities. That is evidenced by the fact that all statesmen in the last war sought to justify such acts to their people as reprisals for the barbarities of the enemy. And through all discussion of preparedness today they find justification in their fears of this frightfulness against themselves.

Enforcement

Now for the moral teeth that I propose for enforcement. That is the definite participation of neutrals of the world in protection against these barbarities. As a part of such agreement the neutral nations should become the referees announcing in authoritative way any fouls that take place.

To effect this, such agreement should provide further:

3. *That the shipment of food supplies in war to any blockaded nation may be in full cargoes under the management and jurisdiction of a commission of the neutral nations*

4. *That neutral observers should be continuously in session within every belligerent country to determine the facts of any killing of civilians from the air.*

The whole of this enforcement by neutrals must be based upon moral forces and not on military force or entanglement in the controversy. Should any belligerent be convicted of deliberate violations, then neutrals should withdraw. Awful as it may be no doubt the hells of reprisals from the injured side would then be turned loose.

The real teeth behind this enforcement is public opinion among neutrals. That is one of the most potent forces in modern war. If it be pointed up by definite conviction beyond all the whitewashing of propaganda it can be far-reaching in its consequences.

In the strategy of modern war one of the utmost anxieties of both sides is to hold the good will of neutrals, or, at least, to prevent their indignation forcing them to aid or to join the enemy The ill will of neutrals or their citizens at once induces informal boycotts of credit and supplies even do they go no further. To influence neutral public opinion in the last war every combatant spent millions in gigantic propaganda. And they are spending it again today.

Public opinion in neutral nations does not react much to the legalistic question of whether cotton is contraband or noncontraband. It does not react much to imperial ambitions of combatants. It does not react much to specious circumventions of such instruments as the Kellogg Pact. But it does react to the horror of killing women and children.

It is asserted that public opinion of neutrals had no effect in the last war Contrary to that, when the final verdict of history is given it will be found that the losers lost not by lack of valor or courage. They lost not by lack of efficiency or even from starvation They lost by failure to heed the public opinion of what were originally neutral nations. Had the American sense of humanities not been outraged over years there is little likelihood that we would have joined in that war. And with us half a dozen hitherto neutral nations joined also. The emotional reaction of the American people upon a conviction of wholesale killing of women and children in another great war would come nearer to driving our people to intervention than all the other arguments in the world.

If this moral standard of protection to women and children were once erected in the world, the violators could confidently expect that the indignation of neutrals would bring them to disaster.

Some Experiences

Incidentally, on Armistice Day in 1929 I made the part of this proposal relating to the immunity of food ships. It was approved by the leaders in a score of nations. Those nations that did not regard it with favor thought it one-sided. But they now find themselves hideously menaced from the air The double proposal should now commend itself to those who then thought it one-sided.

In 1932 I proposed to the World Conference on Land Disarmament a limitation on the use of bombing planes which was accepted by the representatives of many nations. I did not then propose enforcement through organized neutral action as I now do.

To those who doubt the practicability of the idea of ships moving through blockades, I may point out that the Belgian Relief Commission delivered more than 2,000 full cargoes of food through two rings of blockade. It was done by international agreement under neutral management operating continuously for more than four years. It proved that this could be done.

Moreover, the conventions as to the Red Cross were fairly well held to in the civilized countries during 1914 to 1919. The agreements as to protection of prisoners were also fairly well held. At least some agreements to mitigate barbarity have been kept in war. These growths away from barbarism lend hope for further progress toward protection to women and children.

If we wish to lower our vision from the transcendent questions of humanity involved, we can find an impelling interest to neutrals in these proposals.

In the last war the blockade initially reduced demand and every farmer in the world suffered. Then as the long lanes of food from the Southern Hemisphere could not be used because of diminished shipping and the submarine. the demand was concentrated on North America. And the farmers of the Southern Hemisphere went bankrupt during the war. Perhaps someone thinks our farmer benefited. He did not. He has for years and is today still suffering from the expansion of submarginal lands and the inflation of land values due to the high prices of the war

Conclusion

Today's is perhaps a poor atmosphere to make any proposal to mitigate the barbarities of war. So many are desperate with fear, so many have learned to hate. So much hatred and fear are being stimulated by the artifices of propaganda.

It is true the processes which lessened the causes of war and made for peace have been greatly weakened. It is a tragic fact that in six years the treaties limiting the navies have been abandoned. The hopeful negotiations to limit land arms have died away. Encouraging international action by the world conference to restore the prosperity of the world was suppressed. Nations have lawlessly violated their pledges never to use war as an instrument of national policies. Every large nation is arming to the teeth. The standards of living all over the world are being lowered to pay for increasing arms. Fear is rampant. The only methods of peace today seem to be military alliances, threats of force, and delicate balances of armed power.

For America to voice these ideas on behalf of women and children requires no use of force. It needs no military alliances. no leagues, no sanctions. It requires no power politics. But that voice when raised on behalf of humanity can be a most potent force in the world today.

We possess a great moral power and we should use it to save mankind from the barbarities of war. Thereby we will promote peace. In this we will be right at all times.

A section of the convention banquet on Monday night. (See also page 20)

Each Day Sounds the Call

In challenging American youth to answer the call of Christ, the Cleveland Christian Endeavor Convention did not plead for a vague emotional response; *it definitely showed how an answer to that call would require transformed personal life and vitalized group activity.*

Each day's program pointed out a special emphasis of the general theme: the day's activities, the group conferences, the worship services; the speakers' addresses, all combined to show how the answer to that day's challenge could be worked out.

Complete consecration would mean to a Christian Endeavorer answering in some way each of the calls:

Christ Calls to Christian *Endeavor.*
Christ Calls to Christian Citizenship and World Peace
Christ Calls to Church Loyalty and Unity
Christ Calls to Evangelism and Missions
Christ Calls to Personal Consecration.

IV

Challenge to the Christian -- Endeavor!

ONE test of the seriousness of Convention delegates is the attendance at the 8:30 Quiet Hour. It is not easy to get up and breakfast and hurry to the Quiet Hour so early in the morning—especially after an exciting evening and a late bedtime. To the beautiful and dignified Music Hall adjoining the Convention Auditorium hundreds of young people came eagerly and promptly each morning, proving conclusively their earnestness and sincerity as delegates.

"Fairest Lord Jesus" was the hymn which opened the Friday morning service. The Twenty-third Psalm, the Lord's Prayer and the hymn, "Wonderful Words of Life," followed it. Then Dr. William Hiram Foulkes, Vice President of the International Society of Christian Endeavor, whose Quiet Hour talks have been highlights of many a convention, read the closing verses of the twentieth chapter of St. John's Gospel, the story of the revelation of Jesus to Thomas (vs. 26-31). The delegates sang softly "Into My Heart."

31

"Reach Hither Thy Hand"

The Quiet Hour Talk by DR. FOULKES

"The holiest among the mighty and the mightiest among the holy, who with His nail-pierced hands has lifted the gates of empire off their hinges and today rules the world!" So John Paul Richter spoke of Jesus. But does He rule the world?

The human hand, next to the face, is the most wonderful thing in the world. The face is the perpetual symbol of the revelation of truth, beauty and love; the hand is the symbol of achievement. Look upon His pierced hand! Our problem today is how to be courageous in the face of trial, how to be good in the face of temptation to sin, how to be strong in the face of fear, how to be steadfast in the face of sorrow. Christ's nail-pierced hand is at the helm. When we come into contact with that hand we come into the secret of power

What we do with our hands reveals what we are. Would we be willing to let everyone see what we do with them, by night or day, in pastimes and pleasures, at our tasks? What shall we do with our hands? Shall we clench them in arrogance as monarchs do? Or stretch them out as the Prince of Glory did upon the cross? Hands are clenched in violence, anger, hatred, jealousy, suspicion. They are opened in tenderness, penitence, loving kindness, comforting.

Let us at the close of this period in a mystical, simple way put our hands in the hands of Christ. An editorial in this morning's newspaper refers to ex-President Hoover's speech last night as an "impossible dream." But was it? The totalitarian leaders will all die, perhaps by violence. There is only one Lord whose kingdom grows; all others are on the way out. When Jesus said, "Thy Kingdom come," that was not just wishful thinking. That Kingdom *is* coming. This convention is a sign that it is coming.

How many of us have no need of Jesus' hand? Who of us can say, "I can take care of my own life?" No one of us would presume to say it. Evil has never been so seductive, so highly organized, so sinister: it can speak its mind around the world. If we had no faith in Christ we should despair. They who are only nominal Christians live no differently than well-disposed pagans live.

There is only one key to power,—the nail-pierced hand. None of Jesus' words or deeds would be remembered had He not died upon a cross for the sins of the world. I ask you, in some way that will not outrage your reason, to take your hand, sin-stained, toil-scarred, and put it in the hand that rules the world.

"Everything We Do Purposefully Is Educational"

So Dr. J. Gordon Howard, introducing the theme for Friday's discussion groups, emphasized the fact that while the conferences were of tremendous importance, it was not fair to label them *the educational periods*, since every experience in the convention could be educational. Reports of the group conferences are found in Chapter XII.

Since during the two conference periods Friday morning all delegates would discuss the same subject, the eight conference groups in the Young People's Division and the four conference groups in the High School Division were formed alphabetically. The subject for the second period conference, directly related to the theme for the day, was "Improving Our Society Meetings."

Young People's division conferences were held in the Music Hall and the Convention Auditorium. High School age delegates had their group conferences and their own morning assembly in Cleveland College, toward which they departed immediately after Dr. Howard's introductory statement regarding the morning's discussion.

In General Convention Session

Somewhat more informal than the evening sessions, the morning general sessions were interesting, friendly, and instructive. Always there was plenty of time for singing. Friday morning's singing included "We Choose Christ," "Sing, Smile, Pray," and a very pleasant rendition of the "Fire Song" by Mr. Rodeheaver, the chorus, and the delegates. Earl Marlatt's searching and beautiful hymn, "Are Ye Able?" was a fitting introduction to the worship service, on the theme "Important," led by Howard Duven of Iowa.

An amazing story of Christian Endeavor success in a local church was told by Dr. Jonas William Boyer, pastor of the Warren Avenue Presbyterian Church of Saginaw, Mich. By means of a Christian Endeavor Sunday Evening Fellowship, Dr. Boyer has solved the problem of small attendance at Sunday evening services. People no longer need be coaxed to come out Sunday evening, and 800 new church members are due directly, or indirectly to this Christian Endeavor Fellowship.

Said Dr. Boyer:

This new type of Sunday evening meeting has been in successful operation at Warren Avenue Presbyterian Church in Saginaw, Mich., for eight years. Beginning in 1931 it has attracted an average of from 170-190 each week for 38 weeks each season, September to May. *Christian Endeavor* has been used with fine results in this program. We felt that we wanted to be connected with an organization that challenged the youth of the world, so Christian Endeavor was selected as the one best suited to render a fine service.

The hour of meeting was set at 5:30 P. M when the family circle comes to the church together, breaking up into eight different age groups, and then, when the entire fellowship is over, the family can go home together in plenty of time to put the smaller children to bed. The whole family is in training for Christian service. The older ones are training for better Christian service

This Sunday evening plan does not duplicate the other services of the day. The Sunday school is educational in the Bible (9 45 to 10 45). The eleven o'clock service is a service of worship and inspiration. The service at 5:30 P. M is "training for better Christian service," and there is room for improvement for the best. Thus we have a three-fold plan for the Sabbath day.

We begin Sunday with a good Sunday school (except July and August), rejoice in a great service at 11 A. M., and then close the day in the spirit of victory rather than in a defeat like so many churches experience on Sunday nights. It is important to close the Lord's Day in triumph. It affects the work of the chu. :h during the entire week, we find.

The School of Missions runs for the month of November. We use the Christian

Endeavor set-up instead of having to build an entirely new organization for it. This plan lends itself to whatever needs to be done in the church.

The whole family can come to the evening service,—that is from 5 (school age) to 100: from 5-7 years of age, we call the "Lightbearers," Juniors from 8-11, Intermediates from 12-14, Seniors 15-17, Young People 18-24, Young Married People, Older Young People 25-40, and Adults from 41 up.

The hours for this Sunday Evening Fellowship are:

5:30-6:20—Eight C. E. meetings at the same time, with advisers for the five younger age groups.

6:20-6:40—Closing service in the church for all, with ten-minute talk by the pastor, a special musical number and benediction.

6:40-7:10—Christian Fellowship around the tables in the dining room; when all are seated by age groups. People eat and become acquainted. Before eating, "The Blessing" is asked by the pastor, a visiting minister, or some adult

The keystone of the whole organization is the Adult and Older Christian Endeavor societies. When the old folks are interested, the young will be. Parents say COME, instead of "go." This society pays for the cocoa, milk, cream, sugar and coffee, and $1.00 per Sunday for one to take care of the spoons and cups.

Refreshments include sandwiches, homemade cakes, pickles, hot cocoa or coffee. This general plan has worked for eight years. It will be continued for the ninth year. We trust no one's memory, so postal-card reminders are sent to those who are to bring sandwiches or cakes each week. If there are one or two in a family, they bring once a month. If there are three or more in a family they bring twice a month. A committee of consecrated women prepare 38 gallons of pickles in the fall for this Fellowship. We do not eat "supper" but we have Christian Fellowship around the tables for a little while.

This plan has accomplished, it seems to us, many times more than the old set-up The ninth group is in process of being formed and may be called "The Post-college Group "

We thank God for Christian Endeavor and take courage as we enter the ninth year

Dr. Poling's radio talk followed the morning session. On Friday Dr. Poling spoke on "The Romance of Christian Endeavor," after which he answered numerous questions.

Friday afternoon was given over to denominational meetings, some of which began with luncheon, some of which included dinner. While Christian Endeavor is strictly interdenominational, every denomination may suggest to its own young people ways in which their Christian Endeavor activities will be of most service to their own local church and denomination. The denominational meetings are, in a sense, the convention's "family parties," and are among the happiest and most worthwhile occasions in the convention experience.

Friday Evening

Dr. Foulkes presided at this gathering of thousands of young people. Mr. Rodeheaver taught the convention the theme song, "Christ Calls!" These are its timely words:

"The voices of men are a trumpet of wrath.
The tyrants have trodden the weak in their path.
Christ calls us to peace. He calls us to love.
He calls us to power with might from above.
    We choose Him! We choose Him!
We choose Him and follow Christ Jesus our Lord."

The worship service, "Rise Up, O Youth of God," was led by Wayne Bolton of Pennsylvania.

Allen S. Fields, President of the West Virginia Christian Endeavor Union, spoke with much enthusiasm on the importance of the Christian Endeavor society as a means of training young people in Christian service.

Miss Edith Clark, a secretary of the British Christian Endeavour

Hawaiian Delegates to the Convention

Union, was presented to Dr. Poling and the convention by Dr. Vandersall. Miss Clark brought a message from British Endeavorers, and said, in response to Dr. Poling's cordial welcome:

Thank you, Dr. Poling and fellow Endeavorers for your cordial welcome. For a number of years I have decided to attend this International Convention. Now that the opportunity has come I want to thank you with all my heart.

I thank you for sending Dwight L. Moody, who taught my mother to sing "What a Friend We Have in Jesus"; Dr. R. A. Torrey, who gave me faith in God; Dr. Francis E. Clark, who set my feet on a pathway of service. I owe him a debt I can never repay. So tonight I thank you and wish you God's richest blessing.

Miss Clark's keen delight in the convention was to be in itself an inspiration to many other delegates.

Carroll Wright's rapid-fire announcements were always greeted with smiling attention. Fred W. Ramsey followed the chorus selection, "Awake." Mr. Ramsey's announcements at this time were especially interesting, since they concerned Saturday's parade and Monday afternoon's special recreation.

The Rev. Arthur J. Stanley, Associate President of the International Society of Christian Endeavor, spoke with eloquent fervor on the subject, "Jesus Calls Us to See Visions." (See Chapter X).

Dr. Foulkes then said of Dr. Poling:

The Christian Endeavor movement has had only two leaders—the one in whose heart the movement was born, and the son of the faith. There are men whom we admire at a distance—our relationship to Dr. Poling is one of warmth and esteem. Affection binds us to him with ties as soft as silk and as strong as steel. Too many take for granted the courage and caliber of our leader. It would seem impossible to have this movement without this leader who by every test has proven himself to be worthy. I suggest that both political parties would do well to unite in having Dr. Poling as President of the United States.

Dr. Poling responded:

Calvin Coolidge was nominated in this Auditorium! I appreciate this introduction and reception more than I can say. I am grateful to Dr. Foulkes and to you. I have two very special reasons to be glad—first, because of the progressive steps taken at the Trustees' meeting this afternoon; second, because the coming of Miss Clark gives us a new sense of the unity of heart and spirit of Endeavorers everywhere. Miss Clark, please convey our formal greetings and the touch of our spirits to your associates. Tell British Endeavorers that we love them and crave unity which shall result in the power that passeth understanding.

Dr. Poling's presidential address, "Christ Calls!" (Chapter V) searched the hearts of the delegates profoundly. Well did Dr. Harry N. Holmes' quiet statement, after the session was over, express the feeling of all present:

"This was a night of high privilege."

V

"Christ Calls!"

The complete text of the address of Dr. Daniel A. Poling, President of the International Society of Christian Endeavor and of the World's Christian Endeavor Union, Cleveland, Ohio, July 7, introducing the Christian Endeavor youth program and activities of the coming two years.

HITLER calls! Mussolini calls! The Sun Emperor calls! Challenging tocsins sound over a world that rocks beneath the tread of converging armies. The dictators call and youth answers. Unnumbered millions are carried forward upon a rising tide of super-nationalism that threatens to engulf and destroy our boasted twentieth-century civilization.

As this international convention of Christian youth opens, more men are under arms than ever before in human history save only during the actual hostilities of the Great War. The expenditures for conflict have bankrupted human society. By the economic tests that ordinary business must meet to survive, there remain few if any solvent states.

Is there an answer? Is there a solution? Clearly the chancellories of Europe have no answer; nor is isolation, which seems to be America's more seriously regarded answer, a solution. Man has failed. While there was yet time, he offered slogans instead of a solution; he talked about "saving the world for democracy"; he centered his hope in a "war to end war"; he brought forth treaties that divided and sub-divided the earth; but deliberately he turned away from world appeasement. Civilization has again come to the end of the trail with traditional statesmanship, and the prospect is a catastrophe that would wreck the race.

The World's Supreme Need

"What the world needs," another has written, "is power that will make men and women good. Where may this power be found? Nowhere else than in the New Testament." The world's hope and only hope is in Christ; truly, He has the only solution for the world's problem. His Sermon on the Mount is the epic of human brotherhood, and here are comprehended the particulars of a statesmanship that alone can save human society.

We have tried every other way. Within a generation, we have witnessed the repudiation by one or more parties to the agreement of every solemn international

37

engagement entered into since the Armistice. All treaties have become scraps of paper. Leagues and courts have been repudiated; national and international honor are a brutal jest; and might alone has ruled each new occasion. From this world madness the church of Jesus Christ rises scarred, chastened, delayed, but not defeated. There is little to choose between the violence of Russia and the persecutions of the Third Reich. Russia boasts that she has liquidated religion. (But she has not!) Hitler persecutes Jews, Catholics, Protestants alike—more than fourteen hundred clergymen of our own faith have been or are in concentration camps or prisons because they made Christ their first choice.

In all authoritarian states the immediate prospect is ominous, but "the blood of the martyrs is the seed of the church." Christianity is a forward march. The march itself may be delayed, but it cannot be stopped, and "He at last shall reign where'er the sun does his successive courses run."

Christian Endeavor Beneath a Cross

Inevitably Christian Endeavor has suffered with the church of which she is a part. In a number of the states of Europe our membership has been decimated and our activities discontinued Specifically this is true of Spain, where under the free government following the monarchy, religious liberty became a fact and the advance of Protestantism significant with achievements. At the Tenth World's Christian Endeavor Convention not one continental European nation was represented With the return to normal or near-normal conditions in human relations and in the governments of men, we confidently expect a revival of interest in our society.

For such a time as this Christ has come; in such a time as this Christ calls His spirit, His philosophy, Christ Himself, is the world's hope, and Christian Endeavor, in its 37th International Convention, pledges her life, her all, to His person and to His plan At the call of the dictators unnumbered millions of youths march against each other Jesus Christ alone has an attractiveness of person and program that transcends the attractiveness of all other programs and persons It is our task to reveal and release the program and person of Jesus Christ. Christ calls, and again Christian Endeavor answers, "We Choose Christ." With Him we shall march to help make this world Christian.

World Progress

Within the year, the Tenth World's Christian Endeavor Convention has been held in Melbourne, Australia. Here, in spite of world upheaval, representatives of twenty-six nations came, answering Christ's Call. The largest gatherings in the history of our World's Union were convened in the great nation that is a continent The Bishop of Melbourne declared this meeting to be "the greatest religious gathering ever held in Australia." Hundreds of young people pledged their lives to Christian service, the Region of the Pacific was established, and a new era of youthful missionary activity was entered upon.

Within the year, during a visit of your president, South Africa has revived the fraternity of its Dutch and English groups, and strengthened the fellowship of Christian Endeavor broken by the Boer War. Also, within the year, the division in the Christian Endeavor movement of Norway has disappeared. Our two unions, each significant in its own loyalty and tradition, have come together and present now a united front throughout this great land of the North. Should the Eleventh

World's Christian Endeavor Convention be held in Oslo, should this hope come within the providence of God, Norwegian Christian Endeavorers have taken the first and a long step toward making preparations for the great event Within the year Christian Endeavor has everywhere emphasized the solidarity of youth for Christ, a solidarity that beyond all particulars of creed, of denomination, of race, language and color, unites youth in Him Even a decade ago, the church rejoiced in a score of youth movements. They were movements for peace. Today, internationally and interdenominationally, only one of these movements survives All others have gone down beneath a rush of vengeful, bloody passions.

Unique among the achievements of the immediate past is the uniting of the Epworth League with Christian Endeavor in India and Ceylon. As significant as is the new unity of Methodism in the United States is this unity of youth, of Christian youth, in the Far East. Under the direction of the World's Union and with the wise leadership of the Abbeys, Christian Endeavor faces an unparalleled opportunity for missionary evangelism. Here India releases new hope to the world. The missionary church with Christlike spirit and with Christ's own statesmanship sets before the church at home an example that surely we shall follow

Canada and the United States

But India is not alone in the record of progress Canadian Christian Endeavorers report a revival of interest with a corresponding intensifying of organizational programs from Ontario through Quebec and the Maritime Provinces It is expected that a tour of the Maritime Provinces will be arranged by the International Society for the fall of this year. On my recent visit to Hamilton and Toronto, I found conditions more favorable for growth than at any time since the War. Our Canadian leaders believe, and are justified in the belief, that a new era for our society is in prospect.

In the states of the American union, though some of our organizations have experienced fresh trials little short of disheartening, there have been notable gains The reorganization program adopted two years ago has been signally vindicated in Regions Two and Six. Also it is significant, I think, that in these regions our state organizations have been more effective and more definitely successful in their youth programs and with the churches than ever before within the period of my own Christian Endeavor activities. I am reasonably sure that Pennsylvania, Delaware, Maryland, West Virginia, the District of Columbia, Washington, Oregon, California, Nevada, Idaho, Montana, and Utah have never done more aggressive work for Christ and the Church, have never registered larger congregations in Christian Endeavor rallies, have never recorded more heartening achievements than within the two years immediately preceding this convention Other regions have overcome and will yet overcome exceptional difficulties in preparing the way for advances equally great. For them the future is filled with promise and for us all the leadership of regional vice-presidents and regional departmental superintendents will more and more supplement and strengthen the state and international executives to meet both the problems and opportunities of the crisis time in which stands the Christian church.

Financial Problem and Opportunity

Our financial problem continues acute—too acute. Momentarily, it has yielded to the dramatic and generous support of a long-time Christian Endeavorer. The membership campaign this year recorded a new "high." For the first time in more than a generation, the budget of the International Society was actually balanced—a good example for the nation! Beyond a balanced budget, we have found in the annual membership, supplemented by Christian Endeavor Week and Founder's Day offerings, an open door to the solution of our financial difficulties.

While the gift, dollar for dollar, of our loyal associate and comrade has brought what was a dream to the hour of reality, the dream has been given life by the service and sacrifice of our executives. To the point of physical exhaustion, Dr. Vandersall and Mr. Wright have toiled to make this and other dreams come true. My words cannot repay them, and the only reward they ask is the support from all of us that will make their labors more largely fruitful. Our new executives, Ernest Marks and Dr. Paul Brown, have rendered a vital service and given wise leadership.

A modest increase in our income, the increase that we now anticipate, will make it possible for us to underwrite those states and districts that need but a small measure of outside support to conduct without interruption their field activities. Here we have made at least a beginning. The International Society must accept and we believe will accept responsibility for adding to its budget the very modest support that would save entire states from the discontinuance of field leadership and from disheartening interregnums.

The Christian Endeavor World

The *Christian Endeavor World* as a house organ, inadequate we know, but nevertheless serving a very real purpose, has balanced its budget. Certainly the publication does not give our societies the ample topic helps they desire. The editors feel these limitations even more keenly than the subscribers. But the utmost is being done within the requirements of sound financial policy and subscription support. The immediate question is how to increase the number of subscriptions. You may be sure that circulation increases will increase and enrich editorial content. At this moment we are bending our efforts to secure underwriting for a slightly larger and a much more attractive *Christian Endeavor World*.

Relations with Denominations

There is a growing problem for all interdenominational societies as the result of intensified denominational and even sectarian progress. At times our state Christian Endeavor leaders grow impatient with the Boston office, nor do we misunderstand their impatience; rather we rejoice in it. Their concern and loyalty enhearten us. But the executives of the International Society must never forget that Christian Endeavor is within the church and within the churches, that ours is not an authoritarian leadership, that the voice and will of the church and denomination are and must continue to be the voice and will of Christian Endeavor. Again and again, Christian Endeavor has survived and grown in spite of plans and leaders that appeared unfriendly and that may actually have been unfriendly. We have survived and grown because always we have continued to be friendly, because always we have trusted the genius of Christian Endeavor itself, the adaptability of our plan and the providential character of our great ideal to carry us beyond the crisis into yet wider fields of service. Be not impatient with us! Continue to give us your prayers, your counsel, your confidence and your support. Without these, inevitably we would fail. With these and trusting in the Lord Jesus Christ for strength, we cannot fail.

Youth Led

From one of the most distinguished of denominational leaders, a trustee of our own International Society, and president of a great Christian educational institution, comes to me a message that is so soundly Christian Endeavor and that so fully represents my personal conviction that I share it now with you:

"There must be constantly team play on the part of Christian Endeavor leaders with the pastors. Every pastor of a Christian Endeavor society must be held worthy of consideration in the councils of the Christian Endeavor Union and worthy of participation in conventions and rallies. Of course, men must not expect to be called upon for participation and positions which can be filled better by others of their bretheren, but they must be a part of the movement. There must be no factional use of Christian Endeavor to guide youth toward a particular emphasis by excluding pastors who do not hold to that emphasis. . . Strenuous measures should be taken to keep Christian Endeavor leadership young. There should be adult advisers all along the line, but the particular leadership of Christian Endeavor should be young. I suggest that no county officer should be more than 25, no state officer more than 30, and no International officer more than 35—except as counsellors and advisers."

The reorganization plan provides for just about such a schedule. More and more the plan will become effective. Certainly radical measures should be avoided. Sound progress is not by revolution, and always there are sound exceptions to sound rules. But the principle herein stated is sound, too. While the problems of our World's Union are organizationally different, while other national unions would perhaps not look with favor upon such leadership age levels, the International Society of Christian Endeavor is now in position to be increasingly and from "top to bottom"—*of young people, for young people, and led by young people.*

Personal Experience and Growth

Christ calls! And because He calls and we respond we shall not despair. Civilization's path rises and dips. Today, organized society has registered a new "low" in human affairs, in social relationships. But while civilization's path rises and dips, it remains permanently at no lower level. Man was not born to die; he is God's son and Christ calls him into his inheritance of character and achievement. It is the sublime task of the Cleveland Christian Endeavor Convention to help frame youth's answer to Christ's Call.

He calls to personal Christian experience and growth, to an open commitment of heart and hand to Christian tasks. Public service is the reflection of individual experience. Bible study, private devotions, the Christian Endeavor pledge with its time-honored and vital covenant relationship to Jesus Christ, participation in public worship, cultivation of Christian friendships—these are at the foundation of Christian character.

Let us revive the campaign to enroll Comrades of the Quiet Hour; let us organize to bring youth into the worship services of the church; let us enroll tithers—tens of thousands of new tithers. Also let us study and apply the newly developed techniques to improve the worship services of our societies. Throughout the year, let us as pledged Christians be about the supreme business of the Christian—winning others—winning other youths to Jesus Christ.

Unnumbered doors open to us. Christian Endeavor in your church and in my church should cross these thresholds. With pastoral interviews, with guided discussions, with question-and-answer periods, with directed recreation, we may enroll the lives of the young people of North America. We may win them to Christ and to the church, and through the church we may have our part in releasing their lives in Kingdom tasks.

World Preaching Mission

We rejoice in the general acceptance of the plan for a World Preaching Mission in 1940. The Tenth World's Convention in Melbourne was the first international Christian gathering to formally support this proposal as it came from the Commission on Evangelism of the Federal Council of the Churches of Christ in America. We add the support and endorsement of this convention to the Melbourne declaration and pledge our youth and unions to active participation in the missions whenever and wherever held.

Church Loyalty

Christ calls! Calls to church loyalty and fellowship. Christian Endeavor has an ever-enlarging stake in the total educational program of the church; Christian Endeavor does well to give increased attention to leadership training classes and to graded activities; Christian Endeavor believes that every Christian is a teward of his time, talents, money and life, all of which belong to God. "For Christ and for the Church" is more than a motto: it is at once a philosophy and a comprehensive service program.

Christ calls! Calls to Christian action in the community. Christian Endeavor supports Vacation Bible Schools, cooperates with all other community agencies and community enterprises that have as their goal the bettering of living conditions and the enrichment of life generally. With missionary groups, peace groups, good citizenship and temperance groups, with all interdenominational and inter-group activities that have with Christian Endeavor kindred ideals and purposes, our Society is identified in community and nation-wide activities.

Our past is filled with campaigns to promote law observance and law enforcement, to protect the Lord's Day, to stop gambling, to sweep unwholesome reading

from the news stands, to oppose harmful moving pictures and to preserve inter-
racial goodwill and minority rights.

The Challenge of Repeal

"A Saloonless Nation by 1920" was a rallying-call that came out of the Atlantic
City International Convention in 1911. The Eighteenth Amendment and national
prohibition were a direct result of a unity in the field of temperance action that
began with Christian youth. Today, the nation faces an alcohol problem in a new
liquor traffic, a problem more intense and terrifying than the problem of thirty
years ago. A president of the United States promised that "at no time or under
any condition, at no place or under any circumstances, shall that institution, the
saloon or its equivalent, be allowed to return to American life." But as I speak
to you tonight, there are three times as many places of beverage-liquor sale as
there were in pre-prohibition days. The taproom, or bar, or the liquor-selling night
club of 1939, is a more demoralizing institution than was the old saloon. Not one
promise of repeal has been kept; every promise has been broken; every solemn
engagement has been disregarded. Beyond these failures we face the fact that
liquor now is more easily procurable by young people under age and more generally indulged in by women and girls than in pre-prohibition days. In thousands of American communities, beverage alcohol is given into the hands of little
children, ostensibly for their parents of course, but with a constant and devastating menace to boys and girls. In 1917 we were singing, "I didn't raise my boy to
be a soldier," but in 1939 we are face to face with the fact that, whatever our intention, we have raised tens of thousands of girls to become glorified bar-maids

John Barleycorn has not contributed to safety on the American highways, nor
to law enforcement, law observance, and good government. There is a rising tide
of anti-liquor sentiment. In more than six thousand political units, large or small,
the traffic has been outlawed by popular vote since 1932. The end is not yet!

Temperance Education

Christian Endeavor is particularly interested in an educational campaign that
shall be youth led and youth supported. Christian Endeavor continues to highly
regard Allied Youth, in which its own leaders have an honored place Specifically,
Christian Endeavor is interested in a nation-wide campaign to make liquor advertising illegal and to remove the traffic from roadside stands, filling stations and
restaurants. We would particularly commend our associates in Michigan for their
leadership in these fields. A supporting public opinion is vital to any political
enactment; and it is in the field of public opinion that Christian Endeavor will
increasingly concentrate her temperance activities.

"Take private profit out of liquor," may become a unifying campaign slogan of
the next decade.

Menace of the Cigarette

One of the most insidious and increasingly vicious enemies of adolescent youth
is the cigarette. An absolutely conscienceless campaign has pushed cigarette sales
to a point where further increases must be at the expense of motherhood and the
cradle. With secular journals and digests carrying an increasing number of articles
that warn their reading constituency against the cigarette habit, our youth move-

ment cannot afford to be less than energetically active in the field. Here too the International Society of Christian Endeavor is giving and preparing to give aggressive leadership through her state and city constituencies.

Youth is increasingly concerned to have a part in bringing about Christian attitudes in public affairs. We may do something to make possible a better understanding between labor and the church. Study groups, demonstrations, exhibits and the exchange of visitors, will generally bring prompt and healthy returns.

Christian Endeavor and Missions

Christ calls! Calls to Christian citizenship in the nation and in the world. Christian Endeavor is preeminently an evangelistic and missionary enterprise. The Christian Endeavor Society has trained tens of thousands of Christian Endeavorers who have entered every field of missionary service. Thousands of these are today the representatives of their congregations and denominations in all areas of both home and foreign missions. With prayer, with special meetings, with study courses, with the circulating of books and magazines, with dramas and films, let us intensify our missionary endeavor. Let us increase our gifts through church and denominational agencies. Beyond all this we must study the history and culture of other peoples than our own while more and more we have our part in bringing Christian youth into a closer fellowship and understanding.

Christian Endeavor remains today as the one international and interdenominational youth movement, world-wide in its scope and organization. It is both an idea and an entity, a principle and a plan, a philosophy and a program, and it has come to the Kingdom for such a time as this. We must know the facts behind narrow prejudices and selfish national interests that have brought untold suffering to certain races and to minority groups. Without weakening our Protestant heritage, loyal to the Messiahship of Jesus and in His Spirit, we shall seek to promote goodwill among Catholics, Jews and Protestants.

In this field of international relations, it is imperative that there should be a more thoroughly oriented educational movement against narcotics and the international liquor traffic. Here Christian Endeavor has a unique opportunity and a correspondingly great responsibility.

Christian Endeavor and Peace

Christ is the Prince of Peace, and He calls the world to peace. His formula is "changed life through changed lives, new community and new worlds through new world builders." There can be no world at peace without men and women of peace. Because of this eternal dilemma, the supreme, the unyielding task of Christian Endeavor is the task of winning young men and young women to Jesus Christ Himself, bringing them into the church herself, training them for the service of Christ and His cause, and releasing them through all channels of human service to help achieve the new and Christlike earth.

Particularly we commend to our members and unions Christian Endeavor's World Peace Fellowship. Let us enroll at least one hundred thousand members in this Fellowship during the next biennium. Let us be always ready, throughout our Christian Endeavor world, to avail ourselves of opportunities for international conference.

Christian Endeavor Is Ecumenical

In our own country, the Federal Council of the Churches of Christ in America and similar organizations in other lands are bringing the Christian community ever closer to Christ's ideal for the united church. With this purpose and with the program as it evolves, Christian Endeavor would identify both her spirit and her activities. The International Society has been formally represented at the Oxford, Madras, and now at the Amsterdam Conferences. With us the objectives of these prophetic gatherings are at the heart of our life and they are fixed in the foundations upon which we stand. Christian Endeavor is now and has been for more than fifty years a demonstration of ecumenicity. The union of the Epworth League with Christian Endeavor in India is immediately an example of Christian unity that challenges the church in all the world.

What Jesus Christ Has to Say!

Finally: today the world waits to hear what Hitler, or Mussolini, or Stalin may say. Civilization trembles at the threats of passion-filled men. But infinitely more important it is that we should hear what Jesus Christ has to say. He alone speaks for time and for eternity. Christ calls! God helping us, we shall turn from all others to answer His call! At whatever cost, "We Choose Christ," and choosing Him offer our possessions, our talents, our lives, to help make life itself Christ-like. Not a new world, but a Christ-like world, is the goal of the 37th International Christian Endeavor Convention.

"O Lord and Master of us all,
    Whate'er our name or sign,
We own Thy sway; we hear Thy call;
    We test our lives by Thine!"

Glimpses of the colorful parade at the Cleveland Convention. 6,000 young people marched with bands, beautiful floats, and delegation costumes, all attracting much favorable comment.

VI

To Christian Citizenship and World Peace

SATURDAY, the eighth of July, was beyond doubt the most thrilling single day of the convention. From Dr. Schuyler E. Garth's keen and stimulating talk in the Quiet Hour meeting to the last moment of the evening session when the thousands of voices united in the Lord's Prayer, it was a day to remember always.

Discussion in the conferences was thoughtful, eager—here was a subject related to the world's most tremendous problems—how could youth answer Christ's Call to Christian citizenship and world peace?

Christian Endeavor on Parade

Again and again in the colorful parade of ten-thousand which swept down Euclid Avenue, Christian Endeavor emphasized by banners and scenes on floats and songs its answer to the day's question. The governors of two great states, Governor Lehman of New York and Governor Bricker of Ohio, headed the parade, then watched it with close attention from the reviewing stand. Said Governor Lehman:

"I watched the parade of thousands of young people. I saw their enthusiasm, their satisfaction, their determination. They will be—given proper training—good citizens."

Even the weather cooperated in making the parade a complete success. The intense humidity which had made the first two days of the convention somewhat breathless had gone, and the thermometer dropped to normal summer warmth. No need, therefore, for the well-equipped ambulances which were ready for parade casualties.

Very promptly at two o'clock on Saturday afternoon the parade began, due to the efficiency of the Grand Marshal, Major-General Dudley S. Hard. Chief of Police George J. Matowitz led with a mounted police escort. Next came the Grand Marshal, Chief of Staff, Colonel James D. Polley, Adjutant-Captain Perry Geiger, and Aide-Lieutenant John R. Haysak.

Many Distinguished Guests

In the first automobile rode a group of distinguished guests with Mr. Ramsey, convention committee chairman. They were Hon. Herbert H. Lehman, Governor of the State of New York, Hon. John W. Bricker, Governor of the State of Ohio, and Mayor Harold H. Burton, of Cleveland. Mrs. Poling rode in the second automobile, with

Mrs. Helen Lyon Jones of Wilmington, Del., Miss Edith Clark of England, Mrs. Rosa Hewetson Clark of Canada, and Mrs. Catherine Miller Balm of Philadelphia.

A splendid band followed the automobiles and set the pace for the marchers, headed by Dr. Poling and his daughters Jane and "Billie." Other officers of the International Society of Christian Endeavor and Homer Rodeheaver, bowing to frequent applause from the spectators, followed Dr. Poling.

The first float appeared next. Highland Christian Church had entered it—a great cross rose from a white platform, and young people in the costumes of several nations encircled a huge globe.

Blue capes lined with red and red berets made the District of Columbia delegates a gay marching unit. Golden capes and hats made the Golden Rule Union gorgeous. West Virginia had a float on which grew beautiful rhododendron bushes. Marchers in rose-lined green capes and green hats followed the flower-filled float. Utah marched in the form of a large white cross, and proclaimed, "Christ Calls—We Follow." Dr. Paul Brown was the outstanding member of California's marching delegation. New Hampshire delegates appeared in white with red kerchiefs; Massachusetts young people were dressed as Puritans. Sparkling letters announced Rhode Island. Four delegates proudly represented the State of Washington.

Iowans tossed corn to the spectators as they sang, "Ioway, that's where the tall corn grows!" Their costumes were red sailor blouses over white skirts or trousers and red fatigue caps.

The yellow and black of Maryland was followed by the variegated costumes of Kentucky. Mountaineer delegates wore long cotton dresses, reminiscent of statues of the Pioneer Mother. Some did a quaint folk dance figure, others rode in a straw-filled wagon. Delegates from other parts of Kentucky wore fringed frocks representing the famous blue grass of Kentucky. Banners announced that 1940 would be the Golden Jubilee of Kentucky Christian Endeavor.

Whooping Indians represented Illinois and carried red C. E. banners. Very mild, pale-faced Indians for all their feathers! James Misajon, president of the Hawaiian Christian Endeavor Union, carried the banner for Hawaii, an interesting poster map. His bright smile beamed upon the applauding spectators.

The perisphere and trylon of the New York World's Fair decorated the headdresses of New York's delegates. Significant that a former Endeavorer designed these World's Fair theme features! More than four hundred Pennsylvania delegates wore white, with red plumed cadet hats. William Penn (impersonated by William Wise of Pittsburgh) led the delegation, while Dorothy Thompson, also of Pittsburgh, was drum major for the kazoo band.

The Delegation from Pennsylvania in the Parade.

"Dairy-Land" Is Represented

Wisconsin's delegation was very striking. A street-wide banner proclaimed, "Wisconsin, America's Dairy-Land," and milkmaids in red and white checked gingham, with shining milkpails, walked beside a float on which a life-sized artificial cow rode with bovine dignity. (The same cow mysteriously appeared near the quarters of some of the delegates that night, scaring some milkmaids almost into hysterics!) When they reached the reviewing stand several of them darted out of line and presented huge Wisconsin cheeses to Governor Lehman, Mayor Burton, and Dr. Poling.

Virginia delegates carried gay parasols and balloons and generously threw peanuts to the spectators. Long streamers attached to a large cross were held by Indiana delegates, whose banner announced "Youth Follows the Cross." Posters described the international, inter-racial, interdenominational aspects of Christian Endeavor. Nebraska had girls in old-fashioned dresses and young men in imposing frock coats. Kansas Endeavorers in sunflower hats sang "We are dry, dry, dry, down in Kansas."

Michigan featured a Dutch couple, and the Grand Rapids Union had a float on which appeared a cross, and flags of all nations and the words, "Christ Calls the Youth of the World to Follow Him." Oregon, Georgia, Ontario, Connecticut, had small but enthusiastic delegations. One boy marched for Montana. The black-edged yellow capes and yellow caps of New Jersey were most attractive.

Ohio's Own Marchers

The second division of the parade included delegates from the different counties of Ohio, local church groups, and cooperating organizations. Montgomery county had a band. Stark county presented a float with a cross and an open Bible. Cincinnati marchers bore white parasols. Mahoning, Van Wert, Columbiana, and Trumbull counties were well represented. Carroll County delegates had red capes lined with blue, and white fatigue caps lettered in red. The Jewish War Veterans' Band—young men and women—played beautifully. The Luther League of Cleveland had a float showing two deaconesses, an open Bible, and a cross.

One of the most effective sections of the parade was that of the Salvation Army. Its band was excellent, of course, and its young men and women marched with perfect rhythm. A float showed "International Salvation Army Youth of the World United for Peace."

The pretty Girl Reserves of the Young Women's Christian Association made an attractive picture in their white dresses with blue ties. They were recognized as the ushers who served so well in the Auditorium. The American Legion made a good showing, also. Summit County showed dozens of posters giving phases of Christian Endeavor work. Its float was made of white and gold and paper flowers. Its marchers wore gay red cellophane boleros. Cuyahoga Sunrise Union had a float illustrating faith, fun and fellowship. Calvary Reformed Church showed Juniors in the costumes of all nations.

The Baptist Young People's Union showed its interest by marching with Christian Endeavor. So did the Epworth League, with a float telling of its fiftieth anniversary, by means of a huge cake with candles. Some marchers wore the costumes of today, others the quaint clothes of the 1880's.

Practically every church of Cleveland had marchers in line or a significant float or both. Only a moving picture camera could do justice to such as these: The First Church of God's church on a trailer; the St. James A.M.E. choir, announcing "We Answer with Music"; the Crawford Road Christian Church's float bearing angels and disciples, "Ye Olde Ship Endeavor"; Glenville's First Methodist Church's cross of flowers. Bright costumes, striking slogans, meant that every church had its own distinctive way of helping to make the parade a memorable sight for thousands of Cleveland's citizens.

Two Governors Among Speakers

The importance of training in good will and understanding was emphasized by Governor Lehman himself in his memorable address on

"Religion and Democracy" at the evening session. What an evening session that was! Presided over by Mrs. Helen Lyon Jones, the first woman Vice-president of the International Society of Christian Endeavor; made joyous by the marvelous harmony of a great group of Negro singers (the "Wings Over Jordan" Choir); made reverent by the worship service which Emmett McNabb of West Virginia led ably; made thoughtful by Iowa's John E. McCaw, when he spoke on "Christian Endeavor as a Power Toward Peace"; made nationally significant when the addresses of the two Governors, one a Jewish Democrat, the other a Christian Republican, were broadcast.

Throughout the entire session the convention was conscious that here was an experience of fellowship never to be forgotten: the fellowship of people of different racial heritage, different political affiliation, different religious creed—yet all united in a great common purpose, all expressing the highest aspiration of their souls as they prayed together. "Our Father who art in Heaven."

Governor Bricker's Address

Hon. John W. Bricker, Governor of Ohio, made a clear and winning statement on behalf of the practice of democracy as the reasonable, temperate means for government and human development. He said:

Ohio is honored by having the International Christian Endeavor Convention meet here. This group represents great power. Unlimited good to the world will follow your consecrated service

When a crisis is reached in one's personal life, or in his home, it is met by prayerful thought and careful action. The world is disturbed today. Civilization's course is unsteady. Some think we are facing a great world crisis. Everyone, of course, is interested at this time in his own welfare, but tonight I greet a great force interested in the welfare of their neighbors. I like to think of these neighbors as representing the whole citizenship of our America, ultimately encompassing the world. Socially and politically today there is need for funds—mental thinking, a grasp of the eternal truths and careful action

I congratulate this organization and its millions of members on the service which has been rendered. Thousands have been recruited through this organization for the ministry of the church. From your midst have gone into the missionary fields thousands more. Through the membership of the organization, millions of lives have been dedicated to the cause of Christian living, of peace and brotherly helpfulness.

Beyond all this, fortunate is this great membership in the opportunity today, in this distracted time, of serving our civilization. Fortunate also are you in the leadership that you have. I have been personally pleased this week to renew my acquaintance with Dr. Poling, whom I knew many years ago. The joy of his soul in the great work must know no bounds.

We are faced today with a social interdependence heretofore unknown. We live in a world vibrant to every change. A new world society is in the making. No people ever solved a great problem by delegating their thinking to any so-called leader.

The autocracies of the world have scoffed at the church. In some nations false leaders have attempted to mold human conscience and devotion to a pattern. The Truth has been denied to people. Freedom of speech and religious worship have been wiped out. The onward march of civilization toward liberty, freedom and the recognition of the individual's right to live his own life has been thrown into reverse.

Truly, though, today we meet in a nation that gives hope to the world that people of all classes can live in concord.

True representative government should reflect the aims, the aspirations and the character of its people. Your challenge to the leadership of this nation is that it might gird itself with those virtues which have marked the great religions of the world

We are witnessing a great spiritual transformation in the church and religious institutions. They are meeting with a renewed devotion the needs of this industrial age. I have the faith to believe that we are approaching an era of spiritual awakening and moral rehabilitation. A great Christian force such as this strengthens that belief.

The Christian Endeavor movement of the world is united upon the essentials of life and living; upon the fundamentals of religious convictions. You are brought here by the *binding* ties of religion. You have discarded the nonessentials and the heretofore dividing factors of the church. I am glad to join with you in a united move at this time.

I am a member of a church which has on its rolls representatives of twenty-seven denominations. Significant of this age is that unity upon fundamental beliefs resulting in a finer service.

Famed Jewish Executive Speaks

Known widely in banking and philanthropy even be ore he made an enviable reputation as the frequently re-elected executive of the most populous state, Governor Herbert H. Lehman of New York came as a distinguished Jewish layman and statesman to a congress of endeavoring Christian youth.

His message was one of the most forthright and sturdy calls for Christian action against the "isms," anti-Semitism included, that has been given to an American youth audience. The Governor did not "talk down" to his youthful hearers! He brought them a thoughtful but stimulating report from the chambers of government, where courageous men are doing their best to hold Americans to their ideals and their government to its full human possibilities. He said:

One hundred and fifty years ago the men who had fought for freedom and independence drew up a Constitution which guaranteed to all freedom of conscience, freedom of speech, freedom of the press, and freedom of assembly. Fortified by that Constitution they founded a government fitted to protect the liberty of all its citizens. So long as that Constitution is preserved intact, the liberty which the founders of the republic achieved at great sacrifice will remain the heritage not of their descendants alone but of all the citizens of the country—new and old, native-born and immigrant.

America has been endowed with great natural riches. Its citizens have labored industriously to develop its resources. Men and women have come here from all parts of the world to carve out for themselves and for their children a place where they could live in contentment, in safety and in happiness. They have seen years of plenty and years of want. Some fearlessly pioneered to open up a new empire of the West. Some stayed in the marts of commerce and trade. Some built our cities, our railroads and our highways. Some worked in shop and factory; some tilled the fields. Some worked with their brains; some with their hands. Some had easy lives; some found life hard; but together they worked in good times and bad, to build the America we know—a nation rich and powerful, but more than that a nation which in a changing world is holding fast to the ideals of liberty and democracy embodied in our Constitution.

In this country the well-being of the individual is the concern of all. In the Declaration of Independence the Continental Congress asserted that governments are instituted to secure the inalienable rights to life, liberty and the pursuit of happiness with which men are endowed by their Creator.

In other parts of the world men are flouting these ideals; yet freedom, ruthlessly destroyed there, still lives here. The heritage we have received from the founding fathers is intact because every generation of citizens during the hundred and fifty years of America's life has guarde1 jealously that heritage. My generation—the older citizens of this country—must soon relinquish to you, the younger citizens, the duty to guard our heritage against attack, open or secret, from within and from without.

Golden Days for Democracy

In the eighteenth century the philosophical concepts of civil and religious liberty were discussed and formulated. In the nineteenth century they were accepted by all western civilization. The growth of democracy and the spread of liberal doctrines seemed to doom all civil and religious disabilities. The traditional policy of the United States bade fair to become the policy of every enlightened country. Prejudice was decreasing and men who loved their own religion were ready to extend the hand of fellowship to the sincere followers of other faiths Some of us felt confident that the twentieth century would mark the end of intolerance and oppression everywhere and we hoped would mark the end of wars

We have had a rude awakening. In the wake of the World War has come a maelstrom of new-born ill-will and intolerance. In large parts of the world dictatorship supplanting democracy mocks the principles which the founders of this republic regarded as self-evident; it denies the individual's right to life, liberty and the pursuit of happiness. Hundreds of thousands of men and women are being ruthlessly persecuted merely because of their religious or political beliefs.

Reasonable men know that the choice does not lie between Communism and Fascism or Naziism, but between dictatorship, whether of the right or of the left, and democracy. Day by day passion or fear is gaining sway over reason in increasing parts of the world.

Even as recently as twenty-five years ago we could look forward with confidence upon the world of tomorrow. A growing love of peace seemed to bring nearer the time when all men "would beat their swords into ploughshares, and neither would they know war any more." Science was opening new fields for human endeavor and we believed that through science production would be increased so that there would be plenty for all. Education was spreading the doctrine of democracy throughout the world and we had reason to hope that we would soon know a world better than any we had known before.

Then came the World War, and today we are reaping the crop grown from the seeds of hatred which were sown in that war. Today science is used to build machines for destruction and death,—not for the enrichment of the lives of men. Dictators who have crushed all freedom in the countries over which they rule are now threatening the countries which still cherish freedom. In a world which could produce plenty by well-directed labor, men and women are living in deepest misery because opportunity to labor and produce is denied to them. In many parts of the world fear is supplanting hope. National, racial, and class hatreds are dividing country from country, and within each country, group from group. Hatred and fear can tear down but cannot create. If the world of tomorrow is to be ruled by hatred and fear, it will be a sorry place in which to live.

There can be no liberty, no enduring happiness, where dictatorship either of Communism, of Naziism, or of Fascism sways men's minds.

Acid Test for Self-Government

The urgent question for us is how we can solve our social and economic problems upon a reasonable basis and by the application of democratic principles without undemocratic division into classes, without undemocratic arrayal of class against class.

We must prove to our own people and to the world at large that democracy is not an insensible machine of government but a living thing; that its soul is the soul of its people and that it grows and develops to meet the needs and wishes of its citizens. So long as democracy remains alive to the demands of its people, so long will it continue to remain as the only true government. It is our duty and our responsibility to see to it that it does so remain.

And I say to you, who should be the leaders of public opinion in the world of tomorrow, that the prophetic ideals of justice and mercy and love of neighbor are not out-worn or old-fashioned but are still eternally true, that the right of the individual to life, liberty and the pursuit of happiness, founded upon these ideals, formulated in the Declaration of Independence, and guaranteed by our Constitution, must remain the basis of our law, and that the purpose of government is and always should be to secure these rights. . . .

Dark though these days are in some countries of the Old and New Worlds, yet everywhere there are men who still find light in religion; and tyranny itself is forced to recognize that men of sincere religion are its most dangerous foes. In spite of threats backed up by force, even where government is based upon intolerance and foments ill will, Catholics, Protestants and Jews, ministers of God have dared to stand upright and hurl back the answer that they will not abandon the command of God because mob or dictator demanded it.

If Religion Would Live—

It is significant that among the first agencies to realize the danger to democracy from dictatorship have been our great religious organizations. Truly they may be said today to constitute democracy's greatest bulwark against the menace of anti-democratic ideologies.

As Dr. George A Buttrick, president of the Federal Council of the Churches of Christ in America, recently said:

"Democracy is a profoundly religious concept. If religion disappears, democracy is doomed. If you believe in democracy, you believe in spiritual values. Democracy did not begin as a political form, but as a spiritual faith."

In our American democracy we have established a government that endows every human personality with inalienable rights—people of every class, race, and creed.

The United States was not founded to provide wealth or power, but to assert human rights, and our flag means an heroic enterprise of man's spirit of brotherhood.

But when I speak of religion, I do not have in mind lip service or mere conformity with the external forms of religion. I envision rather a national and personal spirituality that recognizes in heart and in mind the universal fatherhood of God and the brotherhood of man.

An attack upon one religion weakens all religious faiths, since the basis of all true religion is charity, justice and tolerance. In the struggle to fortify democracy through strengthening our spiritual life, the ideals and purposes of all faiths are identical.

It is always possible for the powerful to oppress and persecute minorities or groups. But let every lover of democracy remember that when we deal unjustly with or persecute our fellow men, we, at the same time, attack and destroy the fundamentals of democracy, since the very essence of democracy is equality and justice. Injustice to any group or any individual will eventually tear down the structure of democracy itself. Democracy can survive only where there is exact and even-handed justice to all.

If men will only live up to those simple concepts of all religion,—charity, justice and tolerance,—democracy will be safe. No man, whether he worships in church, cathedral or synagogue, can be true to his God or to his country if he does not adhere to those fundamental concepts on which religion and democracy are alike based.

The hope of the world lies not in the madness and cruelty of pagan-minded rulers. Nations which have worshipped false gods have crumbled and disappeared from the face of the earth.

We in this beloved land of ours maintain a strong defense in the two great commands found both in the Old Testament and in the New: "Thou shalt love the Lord thy God," and, "Thou shall love thy neighbor as thyself." Those commands have guided the civilized world for thousands of years. They constitute the soul of American democracy. American democracy will live so long as the commands are not forgotten.

The Holy Communion Service

Sunday Morning, July 9, 8:00 A.M.

"This Do In Remembrance Of Me"

———————————◼———————————

Order of Service

PRELUDE
HYMN—"When Morning Gilds the Skies"
INVOCATION AND LORD'S PRAYER (in unison, standing)
RESPONSIVE LESSON—Psalm 103
PRAYER
HYMN—"Beneath the Cross of Jesus"
THE LORD'S SUPPER

THE WORDS OF INSTITUTION

PRAYER OF INSTITUTION (unison)

Most gracious God, the Father of our Lord Jesus Christ, whose once offering up of Himself upon the cross we commemorate before Thee, we earnestly desire Thy fatherly goodness to accept this our sacrifice of praise and thanksgiving;

And we pray Thee to bless and sanctify with Thy Word and Spirit these Thine own gifts of Bread and Wine which we set before Thee, that we may receive by faith Christ crucified for us, and so feed upon Him that He may be made one with us and we with Him;

And here we offer and present unto Thee ourselves, our souls and bodies, to be a reasonable, holy and living sacrifice unto Thee; praying that all we, who are partakers of this Holy Communion, may find that in this place Thou givest peace;

Through Jesus Christ our Lord; to whom with Thee and the Holy Spirit, be the glory and the praise, both now and evermore. Amen.

THE ADMINISTERING OF THE BREAD

THE ADMINISTERING OF THE CUP

PRAYER OF THANKSGIVING AND CONSECRATION (unison)

Almighty God our Heavenly Father, we thank Thee for this holy hour. Thou hast brought us to Thy banqueting house and Thy banner over us is love. We have been refreshed in spirit by the presence of Thy Son our living Lord whose victorious death we have commemorated. We have come from all the corners of our nation and from many churches and homes but we are all one in Him. We thank Thee for our precious fellowship in Him and with each other. As we go upon our way we would consecrate ourselves anew to the service of our fellow men in Jesus' name. We would go forth under the sign of His cross to fight the good fight of faith and to endure to the end.

May Thy kingdom of righteousness, goodwill and peace come among all men. May all injustice and evil be overthrown. Send us forth in the power of Thy Holy Spirit to do even "greater things than these" according to our Master's promise, who first chose us, and whom we have chosen in loving obedience. And to Thee, Father, Son and Holy Ghost, one God, will we ascribe everlasting praise, world without end. Amen.

HYMN—"O Jesus, I Have Promised"
BENEDICTION AND MIZPAH

VII

To Church Loyalty and Unity

THE hearts of Christian Endeavor convention-goers sang with the Psalmist of long ago, "This is the day which the Lord hath made; let us rejoice and be glad in it!"

It was a pleasant day throughout; cooler than the other convention days had been. The sky was of delicate hue, reflected as a deeper tone in glistening Lake Erie. A day for quiet thought was this—for testing the values to be found in one's life against the eternal values of God. It was a day for the deepening of human friendships.

And it began with the greatest of earthly fellowships: a meeting of Christians at the Lord's table.

The United Youth Communion Service was held at eight o'clock Sunday morning in the Music Hall, whose serene atmosphere made it a fitting place for the Lord's Supper. No church would have held the three thousand or more communicants. They represented, of course, that vast assembly of denominational groups which makes up the world movement of Christian Endeavor.

The service was in charge of Dr. William Hiram Foulkes, former Moderator of the Presbyterian General Assembly, minister of the Old First Church of Newark, N. J., and Vice-President of the International Society of Christian Endeavor.

Others officiating included: Dr. Poling (Baptist) the Rev. Herman Klahr (Presbyterian), the Rev. Theodore Honold (Evangelical Reformed); the Rev. C. A. Hannawalt (Methodist); the Rev. David Loegler (Evangelical).

The voices of youth blended like the tones of a mighty organ as they sang their hymns of praise. The loving words of Jesus fell on responsive hearts as Dr. Foulkes earnestly quoted them.

This service will be remembered by many young people as the supreme experience of the Cleveland Convention.

Convention Leaders in Church Pulpits

A portion of the inspiration of the convention was conveyed to the members of the Cleveland churches on Sunday morning, for many of the churches in Cleveland and its suburbs were the hosts to at least the convention leaders. Many local ministers had invited convention leaders to fill their pulpits. An increase in the number of Cleveland visitors at the Sunday evening session of the convention showed how well the local churches had liked their guest speakers.

Christian Endeavor delegates, for the most part, attended which-ever church in Cleveland appealed to them, some attending a church of their own denomination, others taking the opportunity for better acquaintance with another denomination.

Sunday Afternoon Events

"Lead Me to Calvary," one of Christian Endeavor's favorite hymns, opened the song service on Sunday afternoon. Then followed "He Lives!", "Sing, Smile, Pray," "The Fire Song," and "Jesus Set the World to Singing." The convention chorus, under the expert di-rection of Mr. Evans, sang "Thou Mighty to Save." The Worship service, one of the most effective of the entire convention, was con-ducted by a group of Junior Endeavorers.

"Joyful, Joyful, We Adore Thee," sang the Juniors as they marched up on the platform. Then they prayed, a Junior read a Scripture selection, and then all sang, "Fairest Lord Jesus." Before each stanza of the hymn a Junior repeated a verse of Scripture related to the thought of the hymn.

Mrs. C. A. Berry prayed at the conclusion of this brief but in-spiring service.

From this point on the meeting was broadcast. The Rev. Arthur Stanley presided and Dr. Harry N. Holmes' eloquent address held the audience at breathless attention. Later, a quartette of Kansas Endeavorers—Richard D. Freleigh, Clarence M. Bethke, Herman Bethke, and Arthur Affalter, of the Christian Church Merriam—sang with fine spirit and harmony, and California's favorite, Dr. Jesse H. Baird, President of the Presbyterian Seminary at San Anselmo, spoke enthusiastically of the place Christian Endeavor has held in his life.

Dr. Holmes' Address

Four and a half long, agonizing years in France gave me a knowledge of the utter futility and tragedy of war. Three pictures are indelibly impressed on the tablets of imagination:

1 July, 1916. Battle of the Somme. 600,000 casualties in three months. In that welter of blood, courage, and tears passed away the best youth of the race.

2. April, 1918. Ship torpedoed by unseen pirate of the seas.

3. Australia. Shrine. A population of 7,000,000 sent 329,000 volunteers—314,000 casualties. "Greater love . . . ."

These imperishable memories drove me to give the years of my life to the cause of peace.

We live in a world in which the temples of goodwill and friendship are crumbling and the altars of peace are being overthrown. The carefully elaborated structures, patiently erected for the government of the world by law, are in the discard. Ideals and hopes are being torpedoed, sinking like neutral ships on peaceful seas. The great lights that have guided and inspired civilized mankind for generations are growing dim. Never since Christian Endeavor unfolded its banner have the clouds hung so ominously low on the horizon.

Truly the world seems preparing for some tragic castastrophe or for some new adventure of the human spirit. The nations are not only preparing for war with wanton extravagance—they *are* at war. The power and might of unstinted barbaric force has been unleashed to an unlimited extent Nations are using that power, or its threat, to bring them economic rewards only secured in the past by war. Fiendishly and feverishly economic policies are being used to exploit and loot.

This preparation for war is threatening financial, moral and economic disaster before the firing of a single gun. Ruthless dictatorships are flaunting their efficiency, secured at the precious cost of freedom and a sacrifice of the sacredness of personality. Democracies are uncertain, confused and floundering. The roadway of International progress and ordered advance is cluttered up with broken promises. That instrument of great hope, the League of Nations, is now a weak and broken thing, largely impotent because of the selfishness of the great nations that governed its policies. Established to bring a new order of justice and law as its guiding principle, with goodwill and friendship enshrined in its heart, it was betrayed by its friends.

The idea and ideal given to the world by President Wilson, General Smuts, and Lord Robert Cecil embodied the greatest hope of a shattered world. *Those men did not fail*. The nations failed to display a will to establish cooperation and justice. Militarism is climbing back to a higher place than it has ever occupied in human history, and beginning in many lands to demand a worship that belongs to God alone.

Small wonder that Winston Churchill said recently, "The twentieth century seems born to bring war into its own as the potential destroyer of civilization." Science is ready to scream through the air at three hundred miles an hour seeking whom it may devour, and leaving in its wake a scorched and blackened trail of frightful desolation and horror. Man's humanity to man seems to have given way to man's inhumanity to man. There doesn't seem to be enough goodwill in the world to keep it decent. The dark pessimism of that picture is brightened by flashes of rallying men and women to resist the drift to war.

Christian Endeavor has given two citations to distinguished Americans, both of whom in their acknowledgment made their address *entirely on the theme of peace*. Who can ever forget the moment when Admiral Richard E Byrd stood on our platform at Grand Rapids? Surely his courage and public service entitle him to a commanding place in the affection and admiration of all Americans. We think of him as one of the greatest and most honored of our living citizens We recall him writing in his dairy, almost at the point of death, in his utter loneliness near the South Pole:

"From here the great folly of all follies is the amazing attitude of civilized nations toward each other. A citizen should strive for friendly relations among the family of nations. I feel this so keenly that if I survive I shall devote what is left of my life largely to trying to help further the friendship of my country with other nations of the world."

Then, on Thursday night, we honored ourselves in honoring a man elected to the highest office within the gift of the American people and whose record in world humanitarian service stands unsurpassed and unrivalled. Facing without flinching the dangers of war he flung to us and to America a challenge We must not capitulate to the inevitability of war and ruin. I can still hear him saying:

"Supposing all this is true. Are we to accept defeat of international decency? Must we accept the collapse of western civilization? Must we accept the despair of a return to barbarism? Are we not to explore every channel, try every method that might allay these causes of war and armament and that might lead to protection of the lives and minds of innocent women and children? There are times when to relift the banner of moral standards is essential. For unless it is raised there will be no morals. Because hate and violence have arisen in men is no excuse that we shall forsake reason and humanity."

What response will we make as a convention of Christian youth to the profound truths these men have brought to us from the rich experience of the great achievements? We dare not forget the cost and agony of war. We dare not allow the cause of peace to be a dim red rose in the garden of time. No a thousand noes! Shall we not highly resolve to hold true to the vision we once glimpsed of a world from which is banished the bloody arbitrament of war, and rededicate ourselves to pray for peace, to work and campaign for peace, to oppose war as an instrument of national policy, to repudiate the hatreds and prejudices that breed wars and to rebuild the broken machinery of a just world community of nations?

What answer has religion to the threat of war? What has Christianity to say at this high noon of the world's story?

It can say in the first place that modern science has forced upon our generation a decision for which religion alone has prepared us. Fifty years of emphasis on pure science has made the choice inevitable. Shall it be war and the destruction of civilization and reversion to the brutal law of the jungle, or a closer cooperation than the world has ever known?

When the nations of the world are withdrawing into watertight compartments, religion builds a world council of churches and organizes a world conference of Christian youth, on a scale hitherto unknown. The religious approach to world problems springs from the belief in the essential unity of mankind and the faith unshaken and invincible in the Fatherhood of God and the Brotherhood of Man. The words "foreign" and "barbarian" must disappear from our vocabulary. There is more in common between a gracious lady from England who thanked us for Moody and Clark, although we live under different flags, than there is in common between a Christian American and any gangster of our cities or boss who debauches our civic life although they live under the same flag.

> "I always thought that foreign boys
> Were those across the sea
> Until I got a letter
> From a boy in Italy.
> 'Dear little foreign friend,' it said.
> As clearly as could be.
> And now I wonder who is foreign,
> The other boy or me!"

Religion is calling us afresh to oppose the hatreds and prejudices which breed wars. Racial and religious discrimination are incompatible with genuine goodwill. This ugly monster is raising its evil head even in our own beloved land. The Christian heart cannot accommodate blistering cancerous personal or national hatreds. If we would keep it from dominating the world we must seek to keep it from finding a lodging place in our America. A frontal attack on hate is the theme of Denis McCarthy's great poem:

"This is the land where hate should die.
No feud of faith, no spleen of race,
No darkly brooding fear should try
Beneath our flag to find a place.
Lo, every people here has sent
Its sons to answer freedom's call,
Their life-blood is the strong cement
That builds and binds the nation's wall.

"This is the land where hate should die
Though dear to me my faith and shrine.
I love my country well when I
Respect beliefs which are not mine.
He little loves his land who'd cast
Upon his neighbor's word a doubt,
And cite the wrongs of ages past
From present rights to bar him out.

"This is the land where hate should die.
This is the land where strife should cease
All dark, foreboding fear should fly
Before our flag of light and peace.
Then let us purge the poison thought
That service to the state we give,
And so be worthy as we ought
Of this great land in which we live."

That is what religion is saying if we would have peace. . . .

Before peace can come, nations must limit their powers. Nations like states and individuals must come under the reign of law. It is no more right for a nation to do what it likes, disregarding the rights of others, than it is for an individual to do what he likes, disregarding the rights of others. The next great advance must come in an extension of the great experiment of federalism as it exists in Canada and the United States.

Endeavorers, the unchanging Voice of God, the voice of science and the deepest emotions of the human heart, of the intelligent mind, of the history in blood and tears of the race, of the cry for happiness in life, all call us with abandon to build for peace. As members of that mighty composite we call lovingly America, let us not fail this call of God.

"One only path remains untrod;
The path of peace climbs higher
Make straight that pathway for our God "

Dr. Baird's Address

Why am I a servant of the church? For twenty years I was a pastor (active in young people's work for five years before that) ; now, in the educational side of the church's work, I am dealing with young people like you, trying to get them to see the things of Christ and to get ready for Christian leadership. I wanted to do many things in my life; it was a struggle for me to decide, but I am happy that God made me go into His ministry.

At about 19 I believed the things of the church and tried in a fair way to do the things of Christ, because of a good home. This was not real Christianity; people through the ages have been on fire for God. I believed in God, yes; in the church, yes; in goodness, yes, but that was about all.

Why? I had never really given my heart to God. In the quiet of my room I said, "O Lord, take me and make me what I ought to be." I cannot testify to any great conversion experience; I had been a Christian before that, but Christianity instead of a cold belief became a thrilling experience of fellowship with God, great conviction, and prayer. The Bible became a love letter to me. Its commands, I must do. Its promises were to me for time and eternity. Everything in the Bible was written for me. It became *my* Bible, *my* church. The church became important to me.

Through the years the church has been a gateway out of experience merely physical into experience as big as God is big. Things overflowing with love and hope. Things too big for words. Another chapter. . . Sunday and Rhode-heaver came and set the country on fire. As a spill-over young people in our part of the country decided to do something as personal workers. We organized a personal workers' league and went out to tell people about Jesus. We were not preachers or singers but we were terribly sincere. In a year about forty of us in our own stumbling way had led five hundred people to give their hearts to Christ. In little schools, in homes, we saw people turn back to God, as we tried to tell that Jesus is real, living, that God gives eternity to live for, grace to conquer sin and death, and makes life victorious and worth while.

I came to the deepening and growing conviction that there has never been found a method of making better people that works 100 per cent except the method of introducing them to Jesus. For me any other career than leading people to Jesus would have been stepping down and surrendering the highest good.

Since then I have seen much of the church. I know it is made of human beings not quite perfect yet—preachers, deacons and elders, church members. Old people have a lot of fun out of church quarrels but they hurt young people who have not enough background to see that it is just froth on the surface of a deep reality. Every year has made me love and respect the church of God more and thank Him that I have given my life in His service.

In the final analysis Christian Endeavor must serve the individual church and denomination. Though we move as an army we move as regiments The biggest problem to solve at this point is to study how to serve the individual denomination of which we are a part.

As each denomination become newly efficient, having a youth movement of its own, it is by coordination of Christian Endeavor and denominational programs that we will be able to march forward with full efficiency. If in this day Christian Endeavor could command the loyalty of all evangelical denominations until the whole youth of America could make a solid stand for Christ against the movements represented by the dictators, Christian Endeavor could step out into greater usefulness. If Christian Endeavor commands the situation today it will be with a sympathetic understanding with the youth leaders of all denominations.

The Parents' Hour

Immediately following the Auditorium meeting for the entire convention, the Parents' Hour began in the Old Stone Church. Those who were neither parents nor leaders of children's work had two hours of intermission before the Christian Endeavor meetings at six o'clock.

Any program arranged by the Junior superintendents is sure to be unusually interesting and helpful. The Parents' Hour at the Cleveland Convention was no exception. The church auditorium was attractively decorated with flowers and cool, lacy, green ferns. Beautiful music was an important feature of the program, as Mrs. Richard Gilpin's violin blended with or soared above the notes of the organ played by Mrs. Rita George True.

Dr. Daniel A. Poling presided over the first part of the meeting, succeeded by his associate, the Rev. Arthur J. Stanley, when another engagement obliged him to leave early.

After a musical prelude. "Faith of Our Fathers" was sung heartily by the men and women who filled the church. Dr. Poling led in prayer, and read as a Scripture selection part of the twenty-sixth chapter of Isaiah and part of the thirteenth chapter of John. Dr. Jesse H. Baird then spoke on "The Business of Raising Christians." Dr. Baird emphasized the following points:

1 You must *be* a Christian
2. Play with them Play is the natural realm of children To influence them you must meet them on their level
3 Teach them Teach them how to be good little physical animals, how to be good mentally. Educate body. mind and soul. Teach the little souls how to love their fellow men Make Jesus the hero of their lives
4. Control them. The child is a garden: you must weed and hoe and prune He must learn obedience as he threads his way through right and wrong When the red light shines he must know that under no condition should he go ahead

Mrs. Gilpin and Mrs True played again; then the Rev. Ernest R. Bryan, of Washington, D. C., spoke on the subject, "Heaven Can Wait. Said Mr. Bryan:

Someone—perhaps it was George M Cohan—has said. "I don't care who writes the laws of the nation, so long as I can write the songs." Songs do express popular attitudes. Take for example the song which declares, "Heaven can wait; *this* is paradise enough for me." This song reflects a popular philosophy of life. but it is a pagan philosophy.

All that we do and say reflects our philosophy of life, it is positive or negative. pagan or Christian It is shown in the books we read, the picture shows we see. the songs we sing That philosophy of life has its effects upon others. particularly in the home. particularly in the relationship of parents and children

But Heaven cannot wait. Youth cannot postpone thinking of it. because in youth basic philosophies are formed, decisions are made—on life work, a life partner. life's values. Then young people need a greater wisdom than their own

There is work for youth to do. It is the young men who must see visions. even as the old men dream dreams. The greatest movements have started with young people.

Christ's ministry ended at 33; Pentecost was a gathering of young men; Raphael's greatest painting was finished before he was 30; Shelley died at about that age. leaving his undying odes; Henry Clay was a Senator at 29 and Speaker of the House at 34. Dr. Clark was a young pastor when he saw visions for youth.

There are great tasks to be done today,—unemployment, war, unrighteousness are challenges to youth. This is a serious age in which we live; there is no time to "gather rosebuds while we may." Young people need help. They need to be found for Christ. The future depends on Christian young people. They must have a profound religious experience. How can you help them? What will you tell the seeker after truth? You must be ready to give him guidance, to help him to learn to pray and to serve through Christian Endeavor.

There is much to do! Heaven *can't* wait!

Sunday Evening

"Christ Calls!" Dr. Poling's new song, was sung by the convention chorus during the song service. At every session this chorus was a delight. Phil C. Reed, of the Golden Rule Union of Washington, D. C., led the worship service on the theme, "Jesus Christ, the Hope of the World."

Miss Genevieve E. Park of Nebraska and Ernest Richardson of Texas, who as outstanding local church leaders had been awarded a trip to the convention by the religious education magazine, *The Lookout*, were introduced by Dr. Poling to the convention. To win the award which made their convention attendance possible is to be indeed worthy of the applause they received.

Miss Mildreth Haggard, Junior Superintendent of the International Society of Christian Endeavor, presented to Dr. Poling and the convention a long line of state Junior superintendents, attractive young women and one young man who faithfully serve the children of the church.

Mrs. William V. Martin of Illinois, who has attended twenty-four International and four World's Conventions, was introduced. So was Ray S. Ball of Ohio, who has been a Christian Endeavorer since 1895, and has attended thirty-three State and International Conventions. Miss Clara Dohme of Maryland, previously mentioned, was the third of these loyal members to be honored by the convention.

Bishop Lynwood Westinghouse Kyles of the African Methodist Episcopal Zion Church gave an erudite address on the subject, "What Christ Means to Me." The chorus sang, "All Hail, Emanuel!"

Dr. Louis H. Evans, of Pittsburgh, Pa., one of Christian Endeavor's most popular speakers, spoke with passionate fervor on the unique call of Jesus to youth.

He spoke, in part, as follows:

It is bewildering to be young in days like these. There are so many calls, so much racket, so many voices. Press, platform and radio are filled with offers to youth of kingdoms, social prestige, power, popularity and possessions. The youth of Europe have already made their choice. Nearly all of them are marching, saluting, goose-stepping and shouting for something or someone or other. Not so with American youth. They are following nothing and no one universally as yet. It is just as well not to be hasty. The leader that you choose must in every way meet the demands in days like these.

Jesus Christ calls youth today as the unique leader of the world. Unique in the sense that He has never left His followers. The other religions of the world follow footprints of leaders who are dead and gone, who are never seen again or heard again, after their deaths.

Most of the movements of the world today swing around living personalities but when they are gone—Hitler, Mussolini, Stalin—what will become of their causes? But the Christian follows footfalls of One who still walks with them, not merely the footprints of history but the footfalls of an ever-present Lord. Before His death Jesus refused to say "goodbye"; there was no farewell; He knew He would be back with them after three days.

When Christ calls youth through the church He invites them to several things. First of all, to the reality of His presence in prayer. No matter in what spiritual form Christ appears to His people they all may know that there is no gulf of time or distance between them and their Lord. This is unique in the field of religion. In the second place, He give youth the power that must go with the program. This is a great day for programs. Everybody is organizing someone or something, but programs are not going so well, for we have left God out.

A utilitarian age that has become very clever scientifically has said for a time "Science is my shepherd, I shall not want." But most of our programs have stalled because the engine is gone. The secret of the success of the church has always been in the fact that it knew that Christianity was not a movement but a fellowship with Christ.

You cannot put over a Christian program without Christ. Again the church calls you to the possibility of the character that you desire in Christ. It is one thing to aspire to Him and another thing to have the inspiration to be like Him. The world is full of teachers of ideals. What we need is a saviour from failure in living out these ideals.

Christ is more than a signpost—He is a guide. Christianity is more than a way —it is a personally conducted tour.

Christ offers youth His fellowship in service. In every walk of life men have felt a personal partnership with Him. Doctors have claimed that after they prayed they never knew where their own skill left off and Christ's began. Lincoln on his knees in the White House; Wanamaker praying in his department store; a washerwoman singing hymns at the tub; a football player saying a prayer on the field, and an engineer at a curve praying, "Jesus, Saviour Pilot Me."

Finally, Christ calls you to a triumph over your temptations. If Jesus Christ cannot give a young man the bulge on his temptations at the very first and make him a new man without waiting for the natural processes of habit-breaking and habit-forming, then there is no excuse for Christianity. But Christ can, and He does. He sweeps youth into victories, moral and spiritual and social, which are far beyond their powers to achieve alone.

The call of Christ is still the same. You young people are asked to join hands with a Cause and a Leader that cannot be defeated.

Dr. Evans' address was followed by Dr. Poling's invitation to all who wished to make public profession of loyalty to Jesus or to pledge their lives to full-time service for Him, to come to the platform.

While the delegates sang, "I Need Jesus," over one hundred young people came to the platform. Truly a blessed answer to Christ's Call!

VIII

To Evangelism and Missions

D R. JESSE H. BAIRD spoke at the Monday morning Quiet Hour on "Youth as the Power System for the Future." "Follow, I Will Follow Thee," "Into My Heart," and "O Worship the King!" were sung at the Quiet Hour service. The twenty-third Psalm, the Apostles' Creed, and the Lord's Prayer were repeated in unison.

After the restfulness of Sunday delegates returned to the discussion groups with fresh enthusiasm. The two discussion periods passed quickly and the general session began, as always, with singing. Delegates joyously sang their favorites, "My Faith Looks Up to Thee," "Lead Me to Calvary," and "He Lives!" Mr. Rodeheaver delighted everyone with a solo, "Heartaches, Take Them All to Jesus."

The worship service was led by Miss Geneva Craig of Ohio. Following it, Dr. W. A. MacTaggart, pastor of St. Columba Church, Toronto, and one of Christian Endeavor's best loved leaders, spoke on "Canada's Place in Christian Endeavor."

Carroll M. Wright, Financial Secretary of the International Society of Christian Endeavor, spoke of the evident determination of convention delegates to put across a real program back home.

"To do a real job," Mr. Wright suggested, "you will need something more than just notes. You need something to give to your officers, and you will find all kinds of helps for officers and committee chairmen and suggestions for all kinds of activities on the literature tables. For your meetings you will find topic cards, with the date and Scripture references for each topic, the 'Year of Meetings,' which gives Scripture references, daily Bible readings and a half-page of suggestions for the discussion of each topic. 'Better Meetings for the Young People's Society,' by Dr. Harry Thomas Stock, will be invaluable to you. Helpful treatment of the topics also appears in *The Christian Endeavor World.* The new 'Program Guide for 1939-1941' should be bought for every society. Copies of Dr. Poling's address, 'Christ Calls!' are available without charge."

Dr. Poling's radio talk was on the subject, "Christian Endeavor and Peace."

Monday Afternon—Convention Playtime

There are many opportunities for fun between the sessions of a convention, and laughter is surely not unknown in the assemblies and conferences; but every convention has a very special time for group recreation. The Cleveland convention committee had planned a number of delightful possibilities, all of which were gladly accepted by large numbers of delegates.

Hundreds of delegates took the three-hour boat ride on Lake Erie and jollity reigned in spite of rough water and—for some unfortunates—consequent seasickness. Laughter, song, pleasure in the cool air, and the fine view of Cleveland made the boat ride an especially joyous experience.

To Nela Park went many of the Endeavorers to take the conducted tour through the world-famous General Electric Institute of Light. To see the beautiful industrial plant, perhaps the finest in the world, and the outstanding achievements in electrical engineering was an unusually interesting and instructive experience.

Some delegates drove or walked around the city, enjoying especially the gardens along the lake shore. Others saw Cleveland through the observation telescope atop the Terminal Tower, forty-two floors above street level. For everyone, the afternoon was all too short. Unbelievably soon, it was time to rush to one's room to dress for the convention banquet.

The Convention Banquet

Very pretty indeed were the young women delegates in their long dinner dresses of every bright color and gay pattern; very smart the young men in white suits or white trousers and dark coats. Very festive, if somewhat crowded, the long banqueting hall of the Hotel Allerton. The afternoon's activities had furnished hunger sauce for the food, but even for hungry guests the food was the least important part of this feast of fellowship.

All the executive officers of the International Society of Christian Endeavor were there—Dr. and Mrs. Poling, Dr. Vandersall, Mr. Wright, Dr. Brown, Mr. Marks.

Mr. Rodeheaver was there, bubbling over with good humor. "Mack" Shaw was there, to teach a jolly stunt song and tell his inimitable jokes. Dr. J. Gordon Howard, program committee chairman, was there. "Dad" Reiner, according to the banquet pictures, was there twice!

Miss Edith Clark of England spoke graciously of her joy in the convention. Mrs. Helen Lyon Jones told a most interesting story. Mrs. Rosa Hewetson Clark, charming representative of Canada's Endeavorers, said:

"I am very happy to bring greetings from Canada. I wish that more of our Endeavorers might be here to share the inspiration of this great convention. Our numbers are not so great, but our Endeavorers are very loyal. We hope some day to be able to entertain the convention in Canada."

Fred W. Ramsey made everyone laugh with his story of a governor of Kansas. On an official visit to a prison, the governor, who was bashful, walked along a passageway and found himself upon a platform facing an audience of 800 prisoners waiting for a speech from him.

"Ladies and gentlemen," began the governor nervously. A loud snicker was the response of the eight hundred men to this beginning. The governor tried again:

"Fellow citizens," he stammered. But convicts are not citizens. Again they snickered. In despair the governor made a third attempt.

"Fellow convicts," said he politely, "I am glad to see so many of you here."

Mr. Ramsey continued, "I have met many civic groups in this room but I think it has never been packed with so great a dynamic for good as now."

Only the promise of the evening session made the delegates willing to leave the scene of such an enjoyable banquet.

Monday Evening

The delegates were highly pleased on Monday evening to have Harry N. Holmes presiding. They entered with zest into the service of song and with reverence into the service of worship led by Richard Pfeiffer of Ohio. They were delighted to hear Jane Poling give the youth address of the evening, and her sister "Billie" sing, "I'm a Child of the King." Mrs. Poling was presented to the convention and said:

"Governor Lehman said he broke his rule of not speaking outside of New York State and came to Cleveland to address us because forty years ago at Williams College he had six Christian Endeavor classmates who lived so finely that he wanted to come to an organization which turned out such young men. I believe that if all of our young people lived so that everyone could see that they stood for Christ, the world would soon be won for Him."

James Misajon of Hawaii presented a beautiful lei of beadwork to Mrs. Poling and sent one, by Mrs. Poling, to Mother Clark. Bright paper leis were given to Mr. Holmes, Dr. Paul Brown, Fred W. Ramsey, Dr. J. Gordon Howard, Dr. Vandersall and Carroll M. Wright. Mr. Misajon expressed Hawaii's appreciation of Christian Endeavor and its leaders and the hope that some day a convention would be held in Hawaii. The delegates in response to his courteous "Aloha" burst spontaneously into the song, "Aloha Oe."

The impressive installation of the officers of the International Society took place at this session. The following officers were installed:

President	Dr. Daniel A. Poling
Associate President	Rev. Lawrence W. Bash
Vice-Presidents	Dr. William Hiram Foulkes
	Mr. Harry N. Holmes
	Mrs. Helen Lyon Jones
	Rev. Arthur J. Stanley

Executive Secretary, Treasurer, and Superintendent of Travel	Carroll M. Wright
Associate and Recording Secretary and Superintendent of Christian Vocations	Dr. Stanley B. Vandersall
Extension Secretary	Dr. Paul C. Brown
Field Secretary	Ernest S. Marks

Regional Vice-Presidents:

North Atlantic Region	Kenneth W. Swain
Middle Atlantic Region	Reuel B. Wolford
Southern Region	Charlie A. Johnston
Great Lakes Region	Miss Sarah E. McCullagh
Central Region	Alden L. Campbell
Pacific Region	Albert Arend
Rocky Mountain Region	William C. Smolenske
Southwestern Region	J. Gordon Weir
Dominion of Canada	James P. Godbold

Superintendents of Departments:

Adult-Alumni	Fred R. Roy
Citizenship and Social Issues	Ralph R. Gilby
High School (Intermediate)	Mrs. L. C. Greene
Lookout and Extension	Mrs. Reba C. Rickman
Prayer Meeting and Devotional	Miss Geneva F. Craig
Quiet Hour	Mrs. Dudley Strain
Social and Recreational	Mrs. Catherine Miller Balm
Tenth Legion	Gene Stone
World Peace	Ernest R. Bryan

That the chorus should sing the Hallelujah Chorus at this time seemed especially fitting. The entire convention stood during the singing of this glorious musical tribute to Christ.

Dr. Walter H. Judd was the fastest speaker on the convention program. Impelled by a passionate concern, he spoke with crisp, sharp intensity. This address (reported below) on "Being a Christian in a World of Conflict" was one of the most piercing challenges of the convention, as he spoke of American Christians' indifference and even (by the supplying of war materials and munitions) participation in the war in China. "A new kind of war—not breaking a nation's army but breaking a nation's heart."

Dr. Judd said, in part:

I do have one thing in common with you, as Mrs. Poling said. Some of us have money and some have brains and special gifts, but most of us are quite ordinary people; some of us have good looks and some of us don't. But there is at least one thing we have in common—we have one life to live. I wish that I had two and that you could profit by my mistakes, but unfortunately I have only one and that is all you have. I sometimes wonder how we can be so careless in spending all of the one thing we have.

I am interested in my life just as much as any of you. I have lived ten out of the last fourteen years as a missionary in China. A friend of mine wanted to get the address on his life insurance policy changed and the officials reported that his policy would have to be cancelled, because being a missionary was an extra-hazardous occupation. . .

There are small crises, but most of the time it is fairly comfortable in mission lands. In spite of the fact that they had different faces, different color in their skins, the natives of mission fields long ago decided that on the whole missionaries were more or less harmless individuals, and we entered a period of stability in which missionaries could look ahead to build up their stations and their schools and their hospitals. Things were steady, but now we enter a period when it is again hazardous to be a missionary—not from the standpoint of physical danger, but because of other reasons. The world is in such anxiety, such change, so much hangs in the balance today, that not only just an occasional missionary project, but whole nations, whole ways of life hang in the balance and the solution of crucial issues is before your generation and mine.

It is extra-hazardous to be a missionary today, *first because of the countries to which we go.* Let us run them over in our minds. Every one today is a powder-magazine—some of them already exploding, but some needing only a match.

China—the most hazardous country today in the whole world. You hear it said, "The Chinese have been conquered over and over again and have been able to assimilate the conqueror Although the Japanese run over them now the Chinese will overcome in the end." I hope that that is true, but I don't believe that you can sit down and say, "Let's wait and see how China gets out." Suppose you had cancer and came to me, and I as a doctor would say, "You had *measles,* you had *chickenpox,* you had *diphtheria,* and you overcame every one of them Therefore I think you will get over this" There are men who die today who never died before. That's the way you die.

Previous conquests of China were as different from this one as the Japanese is from the Chinese. In other centuries they were barbarians that came into China and gradually accepted her literature, art, philosophy. With her superior civilization it was easy to absorb and assimilate them. But Japan regards itself as superior in every respect, and to everyone else in the world. Of course there is nothing original about that attitude; the Jews consider themselves the chosen people; the Greeks called all others barbarians Some people in Germany think that they are better than anyone else and I have run across Americans and English who felt that way . . God's chosen . . so the Japanese are sure that they are the best people in the world. One hundred twenty-five generations ago there was sent down Heaven's only son to be their emperor; his line continues through the present emperor, 125 generations. There is not another family tree like that in the world, not even in the D.A.R ! One day I was having tea with one of the Japanese generals. He said, "Why don't the Chinese see that it would be better for us to govern them? They don't know how to govern themselves." (They have done it for 5,000 years longer than anyone else !) . . .

You can't hate people like that It wouldn't do any good We don't hate people who have obsessions On the other hand we don't let them run loose in society either They have to be restrained The Japanese are perfectly sure that they are doing their duty, sent from Heaven. They must save China from conquests, from Chiang Kai-Shek and the evils of the white man. They believe that.

They have been taught that for years and they are not going into this to conquer China and then sit down to allow themselves to be absorbed.

China endured for 5,000 years for two reasons: first, the family organization—everything centered around the home. Both the state and the religion existed for the family, and the center of the home was the woman, and that is why the Japanese are making an unceasing attack upon the women. It is a military tactic which is forcing men to do this against their wills. This is their way of fighting—to beat a nation to its knees until it gives in. This is a new way to check an army and strike at the most vital spot. The Chinese will give up and be murdered rather than have this constant invasion of this sanctity of their homes.

China's leaders were chosen from the scholarly types. When we choose our leaders to govern us, what is the essential qualification? To be able to persuade other people to vote for them! There are 73 or possibly more candidates for the presidential campaign for next year. There are those who have not yet had a single year of administrative office or training. We are asked to name them for the highest office that we have because they have the best manner of kissing babies, or they make the best radio speeches. As long as we make that the basic criterion, we shall continue to have funny things happen. But in China they had the man pass examinations. The leaders of the people wore long gowns and fingernails to show the world that they resorted only to the pen. reason, persuasion, argument. They were learned. They had long hindsight as well as long foresight.

That is why we see the unceasing attack upon China's colleges and universities. It is in order to keep the Chinese people from securing education. We have always said that war is the worst thing in the world. but past wars were gentlemen's wars. They were child's play compared with what we will have with the totalitarian states. You are at a place where you can postpone judgments, but your postponement becomes your choice. We are at the place where no one knows the way out, but we are facing a new kind of crisis.

It is an extra-hazardous occupation to be a missionary in Japan, to embark on one of the greatest crusades of missions of all history. The Japanese fight with fervent zeal and absolute devotion to their cause. Not one of them will be stopped until checked from within by persuasion. economic conditions. etc. The mass of people still will go out and fight. And as to China they are as men riding a tiger. Japan has gambled everything in this war. It is one of the greatest conquests in history if she wins. If she fails, she goes down in history as the greatest laughingstock of the nations.

Five things in particular are the reasons Japan gives for wanting to rule China:

1. Population. She needs more land. Population will really possess nothing by military conquest. It won't solve the problem. The areas that can serve her population are not in China. There are too many Chinese there. Japan has had free access to China without success in getting her people to migrate to these areas. The Chinese can outwork and undereat anyone who has ever lived on their soil. Japan ought to have some more land. "Let her have China!" Well. why not let her have a piece of the United States? We are always so generous with everyone else's territory!

2. Lack of raw materials. There isn't any country with all the raw materials. We don't have rubber, we have reciprocal trade with Brazil. There isn't a single barrier to open access by the Japanese to the materials of China. Chiang Kai-Shek pled with the people not to let their military lead them into such a war. "We need your factories. you need our raw materials." he said. There was never

any reason for conquest there, but this mad dream of empire—Alexander's itch.

3. Disorderliness in China after the revolution. That was a problem in America after the Revolution. Every nation's revolution has been followed by a period of disorder, and China was no exception. The other nations believed that it would take fifty years. One of the clauses in the treaty with China stated that the nations agreed to give China a chance to restore order. They thought that it would take a long time to get straight, but they agreed to refrain from bothering China and to let her get her house in order. She succeeded in twenty years instead of fifty years—from 1921 on, the progress was unusual. China made as much progress in the years 1932-1937 as any nation in the world's history in the same time.

4. After the revolution all sorts of things set in. Capitalism, dictatorship—all of these things were introduced into China as possible ways. Communism, too, had its place, but it passed away, and the communists are reaching the end of the rope. I had first-hand information of this. There isn't any more communism in the Chinese today, in the business sense of communism, than there is in the average of us here tonight. But since Japan came in there has been a resurgence. If this military attack of Japan continues, there are many, like you, who know that to save their country they must ally themselves with whatever help they can get. They have held off for two years, but they must ally with someone who will help. Our own failure to help them will drive thousands of Chinese into communism.

5. The white man's domination from 1900 on. It ceased to be a problem when there was a return of some of the old privileges. China was making such progress that the Japanese Chamber of Commerce sent an official notice to the Japanese to recognize China's growth. But the military came through with its urge to conquer When Japan defeated Russia in the Russo-Japanese War, it was the first time that the white man was turned back by men of any other color. Japan had a treaty of alliance with Great Britain,—the Anglo-Japanese Alliance. In twenty years Japan had risen to an alliance with the greatest country of all years. Japan asked a promise, a clause recognizing the equality of races, and by some queer blunder the English would not agree to it. The Japanese didn't ask them to believe it. All they asked for was the official recognition. England was slapping them down, and almost before that was over our people came along. We were having economic pressure with the Japanese and we passed the Exclusion Act. If we had said the reasons were economic ones, Japan would have understood and not resented the Act. When the reason given was that they were non-Caucasian, because they had different kind of pigment in their skin, that struck them in the teeth. They can't hurt us by their own strength—they can do it by conquering China. We are partly responsible for that ourselves. If we are going to be far-sighted statesmen, not to say Christians, instead of the assistance we are giving by our indifference, we should repeal the Exclusion Act that spurns her because of her race.

Japanese military conquest has got to be checked, but we are partly responsible by feeding the fuel to the enemy.

It is an extra-hazardous occupation to be a missionary in India. And there are more people in India than there are in the European continent, exclusive of Russia. There are more languages. We do not expect India to unite over night. India is a continent settled with all sorts of forces held in control by the moral influence of one half-naked man.

Being a missionary is an extra-hazardous occupation   It is an extra-hazardous occupation you are going into, *second, because of the land from which we come.*

It has been openly dangerous because of where we go, but look at the lands from which we come. We were accepted as individuals for what we were. I would not stand in the center of the stage. Before I speak I know I am of the white race. and they know something about the white race today. They know so well. Your biggest handicap isn't the difficulty in China and Japan. It is living down the uncivilized elements in our own Christian lands. Look at Germany today, the home of the Reformation. You walk today in Germany in a land that says the individual doesn't count. The Christian says that the ultimate value of the individual is supreme. You walk in fascist Italy, which says that the normal state of man isn't peace—it is war. How can Japan and China understand today?

A missionary goes to China from England. The Chinese put such trust in England that when the first test came they gave up Manchuria without a shout. They insisted on giving because they believed in the greatest nations of the West Sir John Simon wouldn't even consider what Stimson was trying to do. If Japan had not succeeded in Manchuria, almost certainly Mussolini wouldn't have succeeded in Ethiopia. and the present situation in Germany wouldn't have arisen. A missionary from Europe is under a terrific handicap What your country *is* is so loud that I can't hear what you say.

The implements of warfare are the fault of the American people Pilate washed his hands. but he didn't escape the guilt of his office, for the generations judge him. We are not free of guilt. My little Chinese hospital has been bombed I saw eight million people. also their homes and the things that are dear to them. destroyed. And it couldn't have happened without the things that came from America. The lines of conflict are 600 miles long and couldn't be maintained without the flotillas of American trucks On the one hand we send missionaries to preach peace. and then we send out the materials to break the peace I see people work in the individual churches to send me out as a missionary, but those same women think they must have their luxuries—silk stockings—the profit of which makes the equivalent of five bullets which your missionary takes out of the bodies of the Chinese soldiers You buy stockings and send bullets over. and then the same people furnish the money to send me over to take the bullets out!

I had to come home The door opens today as never before A quality of courage and standing fast has opened the door—the thing we have been yearning for and beating our hearts out for You can't live over there and wonder if your people over home know what they are doing I can say this bumbly. I am an American citizen and I am not responsible for Japan. yet I am responsible for this wrong program and I can't go on without having done my level best to let you know what you are doing

The *third* extra-hazardous factor in being a missionary from America is *because of the kind of situation we are in.*

Look at the two problems involved which have got to be solved. One is economic and the other that of war and peace Depression, unemployment, economic unrest, desire to get trade and prosperity—America, I pity you. Man doesn't live by bread alone, but he must have it, too. We are so concerned about those things which are for a time that we forget those things which are for eternity We are giving Japan half of the oil she is using to conquer China. and if she gets China we remove from the world the greatest single possible market of today

The only hope of the world today for getting out of the depression with its present social and economic organization is to have a free trade with China with its resources and purchasing power. The Chinese as purchaser are the world's best hope within the present system. We ought to see that we are helping Japan to remove them from the world's markets. Now we can't say that is none of our business when we are taking away our market. We are developing there an unbeatable competitor in the markets we still have. The industry which is getting raw material in China by confiscation runs machines which we invented and sold to the Japanese. It is cold selfishness here to look after our own well-being. It's a new day in the capitalistic system when we build up a competitor who will do us out of business. I don't hesitate to make this last statement: If Japan succeeds with our assistance—she can't do it without it—you will have permanent increased depression. It is because I don't want depression that I say you will have it. The old generation will not see it. It's your minds that have got to find the way out.

What about this year? We are building greater armaments. Why are we feeling insecure against Europe? The basic reason is not Hitler or Mussolini. It is Japan. Their great possessions are not in Europe; they are in the Far East. They have not been able to take a strong stand there. They would have to control Europe. so Japan would be free to get ahead, get possession in the Far East. The threat is at the back door. It's a three-legged stool,—Japan, Germany, Italy. Most people are focusing on Mussolini and Hitler, but the third leg is the only thing holding it up. We could quit giving our support and the three-legged stool would collapse. Checking resources and materials to the military machine, we would stop holding it up, and Japan and the whole totalitarian machine would collapse. Our greatest contribution to things in Europe is to stop supporting Japan's military machine.

Fourth, it is an extra-hazardous occupation to be a missionary *because of the kind of gospel.* The kind *we* have sends us us out not with a sword, but out to the areas of conflict. There is a great deal of conflict in principle between pacifism and passivism. A lot is going by the name of pacifism that is passivism, which is the same as Buddhism. We do not want to go to war, so we lie down. Jesus was not a passivist. He was one of the greatest activists of His time. To be complacent in the face of evil is just as wrong as to oppose it with the sword. We have got to volunteer. Don't think that peace is going to land like a dove on our shoulder. Peace is going to cost something. If war comes, I shall know that it is the result of my failure. No one will go to war if there is any other way to solve it. We are not going to have peace by the absence of conflict. There will always be dispute. Just to sit down and say, "I won't go to war" isn't enough. But you say, "What is the alternative?" There must be an alternative; otherwise they will go to war. If the world goes to war, we must not blame it on anyone, not give in, but dig in to the causes and try to find non-military ways to solve these problems. That's the kind of gospel we have got for our generation.

A missionary wrote. "Does Christ save you from your sins? Then call Him Saviour. Free you, mold and master your life? Call Him Master. Lead you as no one has ever led you? Call Him Leader. Shed light on your way, guide, teach you? Call Him Teacher. Reveal God? Call Him Son of God. Reveal man? Call Him Son of man. Are you helpless, unable to save yourself? Call Him by no name, but follow Him." Jesus did not ask His disciples to follow Him for what He was, but said, "Follow Me." As they followed Him, they came to know Him. We walk in the footsteps of great giants. Our country needs Christ's spirit as do our own lives. We must give deathless, unswerving loyalty to the One whom we know to be adequate for all problems, the Master on whom we may call.

This is the inescapable call of the Christian gospel. Thank God it is an extra-hazardous occupation to be a Christian!

IX

Christ Calls to Personal Consecration

SURELY not the last day! So soon?

But it was, and the quiet earnestness of the delegates was evidence of that fact. It was as if each one said to himself, "I must make the most of every moment here so that after the convention I may do my best to make its inspiration live in my own life, in my society, in my world."

Dr. Schuyler E. Garth spoke at the Quiet Hour, giving a most stimulating talk on youth's part in answering Christ's Call.

The conferences were eagerly attended and there was marked increase in the number of those who entered into the discussions.

The general session of the morning began with the hymn, "Are Ye Able?" which perfectly expressed the attitude of the delegates. It was followed by "We Would Be Building." This is the hymn of the United Christian Youth Movement (Christian Youth Building a New World), of which Christian Endeavor is officially a part. Mr. Rodeheaver sang "In the Secret of His Presence," and the worship service was led by Charlie Johnston, Vice-President for the Southern Region

The Rev. Reginald Kirby of Melbourne, Australia, former President of the Victoria Christian Endeavour Union, was introduced by Dr. Poling.

Mr. Kirby said, in part:

Christian Endeavor in Australia emphasizes the fact that all that technocracy and culture can offer is insignificant unless human life is seen to be infinitely greater than a thing of mind and flesh .

Christian Endeavor works well anywhere—in great city churches, in country districts. It takes you just as you are, with personality now in the making, with incalculable possibilities, and by its activities develops personality and provides enthusiasm for living. This enthusiasm is needed to match the enthusiasm in the world today. We depend for our enthusiasm on the strength which God gives to those who trust Him through Christ

Tuesday Afternoon

There was some free time for rest or visiting with Endeavorers from other places. There were two very pleasant opportunities to learn useful new skills for Christian Endeavor work.

In Club Room A, Mrs. Catherine Miller Balm, author of many books on recreation, and the new Recreation Superintendent of the International Society of Christian Endeavor, gave two complete demonstrations of a party built on games from all parts of the world. Several hundred delegates had a happy time playing these games and learning new songs and stored away their new knowledge for use again and again at home. Many of the games played were original with Mrs. Balm, or arrangements of quaint folk customs in other lands. Exciting march figures showed how to bring guests at once into a jovial mood and group formation for games.

Pictures That Teach

In Club Room C Ernest S. Marks helped a large and enthusiastic crowd of delegates to see the importance of visual aid in religious education. He led a discussion on the use of pictures, both stills and motion pictures, and indicated the sources from which suitable pictures could be obtained. Particular demonstration was given to the slide still projected on a screen by a special projector, the slides themselves either being accompanied by descriptive instructions or by a script in the hands of the leader.

Of particular interest was the use of such a slide film on "The Worship Committee in Action," which puts into visual form much of the contents of the book of the same title, which is published and used so extensively by the International Society.

Also, as coming from the Visual Education Association of Chicago, were several films on temperance education. These were used as examples of what may be done in the field of visual education in young people's groups.

The use of still pictures, reproductions of the masterpieces, and other visual arts were described. The period concluded with a motion picture covering the field of Christian Endeavor, with some scenes of Christian Endeavor conventions and of the headquarters activities of the International Society in Boston.

Delegates Face the Future

Tuesday night's session ended the convention as a gathering of thousands of Endeavorers, but Tuesday night was the beginning of the influence and power of the convention in many, many places. On Tuesday night the convention confidently faced the future. Endeavorers were well aware of the difficulties before them but eager to face those difficulties with courage.

Miss Dorothy Brinkman of Iowa led the service of worship, "Dedication to High Purpose." The delegates sang, "Living for Jesus," at the end of the worship service, as if they expressed the pledge of their future conduct.

Tuesday night was a night of recognition of those who had helped to make the convention a success. The convention committee was present, and Fred W. Ramsey proudly presented each of the following members:

(Chairman and Finance	Fred W. Ramsey)
Vice Chairman and Registration	Fred L. Ball
Vice Chairman and President of Cuyahoga County C. E. Union	Chester H. Remmel
Vice Chairman and Reception	Miss Lois Miller
Vice Chairman	George C. Southwell (also Mrs Southwell)
Treasurer	A. G. Stucky
Executive Secretary	Warren M. Baker

Committees:

Decorations and Exhibits	George K. Meyers
Guides, Ushers and Pages	Miss Annetta B Eldridge
Halls, Banquets and Transportation	G. S. Buchanan
Hotels	R. R Newell
Information	Mrs. W F. Weber
Intermediate	Miss Claramae J. Wegner
Junior	Mrs. C A. Berry
Literature	Mrs. Leila Heath Neff
Music	Earl Evans
Parade	David K Ford
Publicity, Radio, and Press	Ralph W. Leavenworth
Pulpit Supply and Communion Service	Rev. David Loegler
Also associated with Mr Southwell.	Miss Helen Plummer
	Mrs. Stanley Taylor
	Miss Margaret Hinky
	Miss Ruth McBride
	Miss Gazella Hedges

These patient and hard-working people, who had been such hospitable and gracious hosts to the convention, were received with tremendous applause. Another group for whom applause made the rafters ring was the group of Girl Reserves who had acted as ushers. Eight hundred of them had been on duty during the convention, under the direction of Miss Annetta B. Eldridge of the Y. W. C. A and a group of Y. W. C. A. adult members. In the blue and white of the Girl Reserve department of the Y. W. C. A., the long line of ushers made a charming picture as they came to the front of the auditorium and crossed the platform, each one shaking Dr. Poling's hand as she passed him. No less applause was given to the smaller group of Boy Scouts, who had served faithfully as pages throughout the convention.

The Kentucky Endeavorers who had come from the eastern mountains in a station wagon, eleven of them and their pastor, Rev. Lester J. Soerheide, camping on the way and doing their own cooking, were presented to the convention. These Endeavorers proved that the old, old proverb is still true—"Where there's a will, there's a way," to any Christian Endeavor convention!

A Message from Mother Clark

It was a dramatic moment when the message of Mrs. Francis E. Clark was read to the convention. The little lady who holds the history of Christian Endeavor in her heart had been missed by the delegates. She wrote:

Dear Christian Endeavorers All:

Because the "days of the years of my life" are fourscore years and eight, it does not seem best for me to take what seems to me the long journey to Cleveland; but I shall be with you all in spirit through all the days of the convention, and shall pray that the blessing of our Lord, "Whose we are and Whom we serve." may be with you in every meeting, and that as the days go by you may all draw nearer to our Lord and nearer to each other.

I am going to send you as my message for the convention and for all the coming days, a prayer that I once read in Chester Cathedral in England, and which I often pray now, for it seems to express what Christian Endeavor means to me. Here it is·

"Lord Jesus, most merciful Redeemer.
Help me this day and every day.
    To see Thee more clearly,
    To love Thee more dearly,
    To follow Thee more nearly.
    Who livest and reignest forever and ever.
                              Amen."

May the Lord cause His face to shine upon you and be gracious unto you. and may there be something in every meeting that will help you all to "grow in grace and in the knowledge of our Lord Jesus Christ."

Affectionately yours,

HARRIET A. CLARK

Mrs. Aiau from the Territorial Christian Endeavor Association of Hawaii presented to Dr. Poling a fine gavel, bearing the crest of the ancient Hawaiian kings and "Aloha—1939—Hawaii." Mrs. Aiau brought also a gift of $35.

Leis for Dr. and Mrs. Poling came from a little church where Dr. Poling and Mrs. Poling once planted a tree.

Greetings from many parts of the world were read by Dr. Vandersall, and then Mr. Wright announced the winners of parade prizes. The winners were:

For the most attractive costumes, . . Kentucky Christian Endeavor Union
For the best local unit.   . . . Franklin Central Christian Church
For the best float,   The Grand Rapids (Mich.) Union

To the delight of all delegates who had attended the Cleveland '27 convention, the convention chorus sang the song which was remembered with so much pleasure, the Rainbow Chorus. All delegates enjoyed this bright selection with its colorful conclusion, when a rainbow of pastel-colored handkerchiefs fluttered and waved.

Of course there was an offering, and many, many Endeavorers accepted the Recognition Banks, to be filled and returned by September 12, Dr. Clark's birthday.

Then, three addresses, true Christian Endeavor talks, brief but packed with ideas by three young people. Phil Barrett of Oregon, who has *proved* that "We don't like to just sit back and see things happen. We like to *make* them happen!" Norma McQueen of Toronto, gave her message with poise and earnestness. Rev. Daniel K. Poling, startlingly like his famous father—"Let's stop trying to see what we can get out of life; let's start trying to see what we can put into it!" (See Chapter X.)

Dr. Poling gave another chance to delegates who had decided, since the Sunday evening service, to make public profession of Jesus as Saviour or to become Life-Work Recruits. More than a hundred young men and women came quickly to the platform—a second wonderful response to the Call of Christ. Many more delegates made quiet decisions, as they stood in their places, to serve Jesus more faithfully, more bravely.

It was with faith and courage that everyone faced the future, as the thousands of young people joined hands in the traditional convention closing, and sang together "God be with you, till we meet again."

X

Youth Speaks to Youth

THE Associate President (1937-1939), the Rev. Arthur J. Stanley, spoke on "Jesus Calls Us to See Visions" in the evening session of Friday, the seventh of July. His address follows in full.

Two years ago when many of you were attending the 36th International Christian Endeavor Convention in Grand Rapids, Clark Poling and I were attending the great conference on the Life and Work of the Church held at Oxford, England. We were your representatives. At this conference I was called to see visions of the work to be done by the church to make our world Christian. The conference was in session a few days after Pastor Niemoeller had been placed in a concentration camp in Germany because he refused to preach and teach as the government wanted him to do.

Two years have passed and Pastor Niemoeller is still standing for the principles of Jesus Christ and the Church. He stands before the German people and before the people of the world as a person who is willing to suffer for his faith in God and in the teachings of Jesus Christ.· The call of Jesus Christ has been very great to this German citizen. He is answering the call.

Jesus Christ may never call any of us to spend part of our lives in a concentration camp. Neither will he call us to decide whether we will remain true to our faith in Jesus and be killed or denounce Him and live. This call is being answered down through the centuries and many have been put to death because they would not renounce their faith in the teachings of Jesus Christ.

To answer this call takes conviction that Jesus Christ is the Saviour of the individual and of the world. It takes conviction that the principles of Jesus Christ will bring world peace and world brotherhood. We need this kind of conviction in our work for Christ and the church as Christian Endeavorers. With this conviction in Jesus Christ we are able to see visions of the future of the church and its functions in society.

Vision and Call of Church Unity

One of the visions I had while attending the conference on the Life and Work of the Church, was that of church unity which is one of the greatest calls that comes to the young people who are Christians.

For two weeks I felt that I was experiencing being a member of the church universal. I worshipped, studied, and had fellowship with people from all races, over forty nations and over seventy different denominations. During this time I realized what Jesus had in mind when He prayed, "Neither for these only do I pray, but for them also that believe on me through their word; that they may all be one; even as thou, Father, art in me, and I in thee, that they also may be one in us; that the world may believe that thou didst send me." This prayer of Jesus Christ for unity of those who are following Him brings to us a vision and a call today.

The Christian Endeavor movement has always been interested in Christian unity, thus the call of the Christ comes through His prayer for us to do all we can to establish church unity in this nation and in the world.

I would mention six events that are evidences of church unity going forward in our generation:

1. The establishment of the World Council of Churches during the summer of 1937. This came out of the Oxford and Edinburgh conferences which were held during the summer of 1937.

2. The World's Christian Endeavor Convention at Melbourne, Australia. Dr. Poling will tell us more of the achievements of that outstanding world convention.

3. The Madras Missionary Conference which was held last December in Madras, India. This conference had sixty-nine countries represented and was the greatest missionary gathering that has ever been held in the world.

4. The National Preaching Mission and the College Preaching Mission which gave the call of Jesus Christ to the citizens.

5. The World Christian Youth Conference at Amsterdam, Holland. Many of this convention are leaving for this great meeting which is to be held this month of July.

6. A World Preaching Mission is being planned and we as Christian Endeavorers must do all we can to promote this great program of evangelism.

The call of Jesus Christ to Christian Endeavor is to aid all Christians in striving to answer His prayer, "That all might be one." When we answer this call as we do in our Christian Endeavor movement we see visions of what the church can do to help solve the baffling problems of the world.

Vision and Call of World Brotherhood

The second vision to which Jesus Christ calls us today is world brotherhood. This vision seems almost impossible when one reads the newspapers and listens to the radio. It is possible when we follow the teachings of Jesus Christ. For all men are created equal and Christ calls all men to follow Him and to accept God as their Father, and when people answer this call there will be world brotherhood.

When I was attending the University of Oregon we had a peace parade. In this parade was a slogan, "The 19th century has made the world a neighborhood; it is the task of the 20th century to make the world a brotherhood."

This would be a good slogan for some state union or some other group to carry in our parade tomorrow afternoon. At the present time the youth of the world are on the "39-yard line and they have 61 yards" to go before the end of the century. The goal is certainly a challenge and a call to the youth of every generation of the 20th century and especially is this true of the Christian youth of the world.

Let us now as Christian Endeavorers living in a nation that maintains freedom of worship and believing in brotherhood answer this call by doing all we can as individuals and as C. E. societies and C. E. unions to establish brotherhood in our dealings with China, Germany, and other countries. One of our religious leaders has said, "We can do much for peace by helping the refugees. Let the world know we believe." The Christian Endeavorers of China are aiding their refugees. We will be interested in those of another nationality and of other races. We will aid others as Christian Endeavorers.

We should do all we can as young people to help in the missionary work of our churches so the message of Christian brotherhood may reach everyone in the world. We can make our missionary work more interesting if we take time and make the effort to discover what missions have done and are doing. Some of the most interesting reading we have is found in the books written by missionaries.

Many Christian Endeavorers' have answered the call of Jesus to service in missionary work. They had answered the call of Jesus Christ by going to some home or foreign missionary field. All of us need to answer this call by being interested in the work of the missionaries, by giving to mission work, and some of us should follow other Christian Endeavorers into Christian missionary service.

When we dedicate ourselves to the task of making this world a brotherhood during our generation we will answer the call of Jesus to be a brother of all mankind and in so doing we will see visions of a world won to Jesus Christ and a world in which nations would live together peacefully.

This vision is possible when the youth of the world realize that the teaching of Jesus Christ concerning love and winning others to His cause is the supreme need of this time. Many youth of our generation do not know that this is true: therefore, those of us who know that Christianity has the solution of our world problems must take the teachings of Jesus Christ to the youth of our own communities first, and then to those youth of other races and nationalities. This is the great commission of our generation and it is the same as the commission given to the disciples by Jesus Christ.

Christ Calls Us to a Vision of Unselfishness

Recently a drive was made in the Philippines to raise money for the refugees of China. A small boy heard about the Chinese children suffering and being homeless. He had been saving his money for a bicycle. He took this money which he had saved and purchased a great sack of bread, so large that he had to drag it to the headquarters of the refugee fund. Those in charge did not know what to do because the bread could not be shipped to the refugee children in China. Someone suggested that they sell the loaves to the members of the civic clubs as they met for their noon luncheons. This was done and they were able to send many more things to the refugees. This is similar to the little boy who had five loaves and two fishes; he gave all that he had so Jesus could feed the great multitude. The boy in the Philippines gave all that he had and it was increased to aid others.

Christ calls us to unselfish service. We may answer this call in everything in life, in our work in Christian Endeavor, in our school life, in our home life, and in the work we do to make a living. When we answer this call we are able to see the vision of a Christian community and a Christian world.

The Call of Christ Is Totalitarian

We are living in a day when our world leaders demand that their followers devote themselves to them in every way. It is a day of totalitarianism. It is a day of giving our all to some leader or cause. For Christian Endeavorers, the leader is Jesus Christ and the cause is Christianity.

This call came to the disciples. They gave up all that they might serve Him during their lifetime. Since that time when Jesus called the fishermen from the Sea of Galilee, men and women have given themselves to Jesus in a totalitarian way and we inherit their labors and accomplishments to carry on to greater things than these.

Communism calls youth of Russia to build a new Russia.
Fascism calls the youth of Italy to build a new Italy.
Hitler calls the youth of Germany to build a new Germany.

Jesus Christ calls the youth of the entire world to build a Christian world. Let us answer His call and give ourselves to Him in service and worship.

We are partners with God in building a Christian world Let us fulfill our part of this partnership.

The vision of giving ourselves completely to the teachings of Jesus Christ and answering His call without any reservations is the greatest vision of this age

I want to share another experience with this convention. Last year I had the privilege of being a speaker at the Kansas State Christian Endeavor Convention in Wichita. I was speaking in the First Presbyterian Church. Those of you who have been in this church will remember the lovely stained glass window on the left side of the church. It is the picture of the Ascension. Jesus is in the upper part and the disciples are in the lower part. At the bottom were the words, "Lo, I am with you always." As I looked at the window I could see the audience below the disciples. To me it made those words of Jesus mean more than they had ever meant The disciples had answered His call and were now ready to go out in the world to do the work that He had given them. Can we picture ourselves tonight as followers of Jesus Christ, ready to answer His call in all things of life, so that others may accept Jesus as their leader and Saviour? So the Gospel of Jesus Christ and the work of the church will go forward with our help?

Let us answer the call of Jesus Christ to see visions of church unity, world brotherhood, unselfish service and Christian totalitarianism, to do all in our power and with the help of our God move forward in our work for the church

Trusting in the Lord Jesus Christ for strength we can see these visions and answer the call of Jesus Christ!

Other Eloquent Youth Leaders

An outstanding feature of the Cleveland Convention was the active participation of many other young Christian Endeavorers, in the sessions day by day. Young men and young women led each of the worship services with which the general sessions began. Youth speakers clearly expressed their ideals and ideas in clear and dignified platform addresses.

Those who led the worship services included Miss Blanche Yeomans of Kansas, Howard Duven of Iowa, Wayne Bolton of Pennsylvania, Phil C. Reed of the Golden Rule Union, Washington, D. C., Miss Geneva Craig of Ohio, Charlie Johnston, Regional Vice-President of the Southern Region, Emmett McNabb of West Virginia, Richard Pfeiffer of Ohio, and Miss Dorothy Brinkman of Iowa.

All the services of worship were helpful and inspiring. All were carefully planned in advance. There was no "speech making" here; only an occasional word on the part of the leader to guide the thinking of the group. For example, Miss Geneva Craig of Ohio prefaced a unison praying of the Lord's Prayer with these words:

When we say "Our" Father, as Jesus taught His disciples to pray, all mankind is included. This is difficult for many of us to believe, but this is the threshold over which all of us must step before we can pray the Lord's Prayer. Jesus included the world as His brothers. His prayer was for all creatures.

And when He had finished praying "Thy kingdom come," He went out and helped it to come. Action follows effective prayer as surely as the sun rises. So are we going to sit idly by and just repeat those words and not mean them, or are we too going to go out from this convention and help make "Thy kingdom come"?

Brief addresses were made by a number of young men and women. Space limitations prevent the inclusion of all of them in this report. But some typical addresses are given here.

Christian Endeavor as a Power Toward World Peace

By John E. McCaw, Des Moines, Iowa, Executive Secretary, Iowa Christian Endeavor Union.

It never before occurred to me to consider Christian Endeavor as a *power* toward world peace. To me Christian Endeavor was more to be considered as an influence toward peace, but the word "influence" seems dwarfed beside the word "power." Power denotes not only influence and action but also a tremendous potentiality. Christian Endeavor in truth is more than an influence. It *is* a power and as such its great potentialities challenge us to utilize that power.

Christian Endeavor in its very composition proves its right to be called a power for world peace. It is international in scope; it is not bound by national boundaries; it transcends nationalism. The very presence in this convention of delegates from the nations of the North American continent and the gracious presence of delegates from Great Britain and Australasia give proof to the internationalism of Christian Endeavor.

The World Convention of Christian Endeavor provides further evidence of the internationalism of Christian Endeavor In Melbourne, Australia, last summer over twenty-four nations were represented in the traditional exchange of flags in the flag parade. To witness such a spectacle where the representatives from each nation march with their flags to the front, there exchange them with one another to show their unity in Christian Endeavor, is indeed to witness a testimony to the internationalism of Christian Endeavor

Christian Endeavor in its inter-racial aspects also makes a definite contribution toward world peace. In the world today there are tendencies to misunderstand other races and cultures as well as the tendency to make God a tribal god. However, to the Christian Endeavorers around the world there is only one God and the same God In Christian Endeavor there are no minorities, no blood that gives superiority, no allegiance as great as the allegiance to Christ and His program.

In the educational aspects of Christian Endeavor a vast power for world peace is exerted. Christian Endeavorers participate in the World Peace Fellowship. In this Fellowship Christian Endeavor participates in the peace councils of the world. Many of the Sunday evening topics during the year have a direct as well as indirect bearing on peace and international relationships. The new Program Guide issued at this convention calls for observance of such days as World Goodwill Day, Armistice Day, and the World Day of Prayer.

Christian Endeavor by its very name must in order to be consistent and loyal to the teachings of the Prince of Peace be a power toward world peace. Loyalty to such a leader and such a kingdom program not only makes Christian Endeavor a power for world peace but also makes individual Endeavorers, whether American, Canadian, Korean, German, or British, responsible for the living of lives in harmony with the Great Leader and Master, Jesus Christ.

Youth Facing Modern Problems

By Mrs. Norma McQueen, Hamilton, Ontario

The problems which confront youth today are twofold,—first, his own personal problems; and, secondly, those which relate to other persons and the world generally. It is not possible for us, as Christian youth, to face one without facing the other. If we would concentrate upon our own personal problems to the exclusion of those about us or the world at large, we would indeed become selfish and self-centered, and certainly not worthy to be called followers of Christ; but, if we seek to interest ourselves in the problems of others, and the world generally, we will find ourselves nearer to the solution of our own.

The problems which we face are not entirely new to young people but I truly believe that we are being called upon to shoulder our responsibilities more definitely than was any generation before us. The countries of the world today are looking, as never before, to the youth of their lands to undertake tasks of tremendous importance.

Youth today is capable of very sane, serious thinking and logical reasoning The means of communication today (radio, newspapers, moving pictures) are responsible to a great degree for the fact that youth is far better informed than past generations on subjects of great importance, and we find young people expressing themselves freely and intelligently on any number of subjects pertaining to affairs of national and international significance. And yet we do find youth in a confusion of thought on certain subjects. For instance, we find many young people who have become confused regarding religion. They say, "There are so many beliefs, what am I to believe?" It is unfortunately true that radical propaganda is appealing to some young people today because it seems to offer an easy way of life. It is possible that Christianity has been misunderstood through the lack of proper emphasis being placed on it Christ is OUR EXAMPLE in both life and character, but unless we ourselves manifest such an example, how can we hope to bring others to Christ? Must we desert our highest ideals and make concessions? No' We must stick to the Gospel of Jesus Christ We must be sure that the structure we are building on the foundation already prepared for us is worthy of the principles of Christ and Christian Endeavor.

There is a story told of a certain minister who had watched a parade of young Socialists of the Purple Shirt, and after the parade had passed he was heard to say, "These Communist and Socialist youth likely believe that they can turn the world upside down, but our Christian youth don't" Is that not a CHALLENGE to us? *We must have the courage of our convictions!*

The young people of the United States and Canada stress the need of "World Friendship" while in many countries the young people are being filled with nationalistic propaganda. It has been truly said by our beloved monarch, King George VI, following his recent visit with our gracious Queen Elizabeth to our countries that "the United States and Canada are indeed an example to the rest of the world." Our youth, realizing the futility of war, can logically defend their positions, whether it be that of the pacifist, or the support of governmental program, cost what it may! The same is also true of the attitude of our youth towards race prejudice and class dictinction, and the great desire of our youth is that this world of ours may become a peaceful neighborhood in which to live!

As youth today we are called upon to take a very definite stand regarding the moral problems of this day. Moral leaders are today asking the church to "do something about it." The standard of morals set for us by Jesus is the only standard by which we should measure the morals of any life. We should not accentuate man's faults or worthlessness, but rather be ready and willing to give him a lift. Dr. George MacDonald, the eminent Scottish preacher, during his ministry came upon a woman who was morally degraded. He invited her to his study in his home to try and give her some spiritual help. His young son, upon seeing the woman enter the study, asked his mother, "Who is in the study with Daddy?" His mother replied, "It is an angel who has lost her way, son, and Daddy is going to try and help her find her way back again." Such sympathy and understanding can only reveal a Christlike character.

This might well be termed the "Golden Age" of youth; for the opportunities which are given to us, and the possibilities which lie before us, are challenging us to answer the Call of Christ. Christian youth is ready to do its part in dealing with modern problems, and on this closing night of this wonderful convention, may we accept this challenge personally, and surrender our lives wholeheartedly to Christ and to His service in facing up to these problems ably and courageously.

We will stay through!

What Has Christ to Offer the Youth of Today?

By Phil W. Barrett, Vice-President, Oregon Christian Endeavor Union

When we appraise a movement which we have been called to join we usually ask the question, "What has it to offer me?"—and we have a perfect right to ask that. As young people we are called upon to make many decisions, some of which require little thought, others which require time and study, but we still have to make these decisions.

Christ has called us to make a decision to follow Him. "Christ calls us," and we then, since the decision is in our own hands, have the right and privilege of asking, "What has Christ to offer me?"

There are so many things that Christ has to offer that we cannot possibly enumerate them tonight. Yet there are a few which it would be well to think about

First of all, He offers us inspiration. No man is a leader who cannot inspire his followers to reach a definite goal. A leader without personality and enthusiasm which go to make up inspiration is seldom successful or seldom found. So Christ offers us more inspiration than we are accustomed to find in the leaders of people today. He inspires us to greater heights. We are inspired by His works, by His actions, and by the way He challenges lives, and as He stands before us tonight He offers us His great inspiration. But we need something more than just being inspired. We need something definite to be inspired about.

And so after inspiration we find that Christ offers us possibilities for spiritual and moral leadership. We sometimes say of young people, "My! What possibilities he or she has!" And yet we say that the young person who has let Christ come into his life has greater possibilities for leadership or for anything else, for that matter, than one who does not know Christ or what He has to offer.

No other person, no other movement can offer us so great or so many possibilities.

And as Christ calls us today we find a great possibility for spiritual or moral leadership.

Now we are thinking what Christ has to offer the youth of today. All youth unfortunately do not care about Christ or what He has to offer, and so we must think of a challenging thought that, in order for all the youth to know Christ, He must have us offer them. He must have each one of us, whoever we are, whatever we do. He must be able to say to us, "Show Me to that fellow or girl. Let Me shine through your life so that they will see Me." Christ has been calling us in this convention. He calls us now that He may offer us as ambassadors to the youth of today.

And finally, Christ offers Himself and that is a challenge. We say of a young person, "He or she has everything," and yet sometimes there is lacking the greatest essential for life. Christ is the only one who really has everything. He has more to offer than Hitler, Mussolini, or Stalin. He is more alive than a Confucius or Mohammed. He stands today before us and offers us a challenge. "I call. Will you follow?" The challenge today is as great as it was when He took Matthew, the tax-gatherer, from the doorstep of the counting-house. It is even greater to us because it includes us in that challenge and our answer tonight as we close a time of wonderful fellowship and working together is, "We choose Christ." We choose Him to take over our hearts and lives, and each one of us, when we think of what Christ has to offer the youth of today, feels that, including ourselves, Christ has everything.

What Is Today's Challenge?

By Rev. Daniel K. Poling

The following story is one of history's treasures. I remember hearing it first some years ago. It is found in the account of the battle of Sempach fought between the Swiss and the Austrians in A. D. 1386. Things were going hard with the Swiss. The Austrian forces of several thousand were rapidly surrounding them with a "living wall of steel." At the moment when despair was about to sweep over the defending army a brave knight of Unterwalden resolved to sacrifice his life for his country. Calling out to his comrades, "Dear brothers, I will open a way for you," he rushed toward the Austrian lines. When he reached them he seized as many of the pointed lances of the armored knights as he could grasp and plunged them into his body with the cry, "Make way for liberty." His fellows, caught by the spirit of his sacrifice, followed. They rushed through the opening in the Austrian ranks made by the hero, and fought so vigorously that the tide was turned and a decisive victory was won.

"Spear Thrusts Into Life" hurt and sometimes they cause death. But generally when the spirit of sacrifice is present "Spear Thrusts Into Life" do good.

Arnold Winkelried, that was his name, for the sake of home and country received into his body the spears of the enemy. These spears took his life but they made possible the freedom of his countrymen.

And we must understand that the world today is full of sharp and pointed spears which command us to do their masters' bidding. Unless we take their wounds we shall become the slaves of whatever commands us.

We must learn to stand mental and physical pain as well as pains of desire. This is something which too few do, either for the sake of others or for the sake of self. Rather than stand up against the spears and endure their cut they surrender and go down in failure because it is the least exacting way.

Very likely your class in high school or college was an example of what I mean. My class was and every class I know has been. When you started as Freshmen, was it not true that your number was larger than it was the day of your graduation? If not, it was certainly true that there were some in the class then who did not graduate in four years. What happened to them? We do not include those who may have been forced to give up their education because of need at home or sickness or for some other necessary reason. Excluding these, am I not correct in saying that there were some who gave up because the winter was too cold or the discipline too strict or the subjects too hard, or the students too rough? In other words they were not willing to make the sacrifice necessary to obtain an education. It isn't easy to earn a diploma. Much of the necessary procedure is difficult and some are not willing to stand up under it. They choose the easy way and surrender before the spears which say "Give up, or else it will hurt." Remember it's the hurt that does the good. Bear the pain of an education today and in the future you may be a doctor, teacher, preacher or, not least among men, an intelligent ditch digger. But no matter what you turn out to be, you will always have the satisfaction of knowing and others will know that you were able to complete what you set out to do.

You know as I do that one of the greatest problems that men and women face today is the problem of intemperance One can be intemperate with most anything. He can eat too much, sleep too much, or wear too often a red necktie. Excess is the ruination of thousands. Students read too much and get nervous breakdowns, they fall too deeply in love and commit suicide, they play too much and fail in school. But when intemperance is mentioned we quite naturally think of the use of intoxicating liquor. For the word is most generally used in this connection.

Today beer, ale and whisky are advertised everywhere. Their merits are proclaimed from printed page, billboard, and radio. Confronted by this "living wall of steel" thousands surrender before the threat of give up, or else we will ostracize you, ruin your business, cause you to lose your job, make you unpopular. To say no in the face of so mighty a voice is difficult. It takes courage and will power. It requires great sacrifice. Above all it hurts. These spears will pierce you if you refuse. It is easy to give in. But if you do your future may be clouded with drunkenness, a broken home, children's hatred, loss of job and disgrace. Whereas if you stand out and endure the open wounds inflicted by them your future will be rich in self-respect and public esteem. The poorest individual can win the respect of his community while the richest can be despised.

XI

Typical Radio Conference

E ACH morning at 12:30 Dr. Poling spoke to the convention and to the radio audience on some timely and interesting theme. These radio talks and the questions and answers which followed them extended the influence of the convention to the entire continent. A typical radio talk and the questions and answers which followed it are given here.

What About Youth—Good, Bad or Indifferent?

A few years ago I sat with a clergyman, not far from Albany, the capital city of New York. I delivered an address at the youth meeting This clergyman said to me, as we faced the fire together that night, "Call me a coward if you wish, but deliberately I would not be a father. I would not want to have any responsibility or any share in responsibility of bringing a new life into the world." He talked to me about conditions in our society that made him feel justified in saying that. He talked about the extreme lives of many young people He went on with deep feeling and that was all the text of what he had to say. Then he held before my eyes the *Knickerbocker-Press* and on the front page of that paper was the story of a party that had been held the night before in which a young person had died—a story of wild excesses, a story of high school young people who had done the wrong thing.

Always a few misrepresent the many and always the few are responsible for the headlines—the few who live the wrong kind of life I said it was unfair to bring a general indictment against bankers because one banker defaulted It was unfair to bring a general indictment against all merchants because some merchants have short-changed you. I told him it was unfair and grossly unfair to condemn all the clergymen, priests, and rabbis in the country because one clergyman, priest, or rabbi forgets his vows. I told him it was unfair to bring a general indictment again t all young people.

Within two or three days after the issue of that paper a student in that school made the statement that only nine young people were represented in that sad affair and that not all nine young people were in that school and that it was unfair and unjust and untrue to have a story on the front page of a newspaper that brought discredit to over 1,800 boys and girls and young men and women Always, I say, the few misrepresent the many.

One man who makes a noise makes more noise than 10,000 men who make no noise at all.

I am not here to defend young people who do the wrong thing, but I am here to say that youth in my time—young men and young women—are as intrinsically fine and worthy as young people have ever been, and I think I know young people. Eight children have been bringing me up in the way I should go for a good many years. If we do not talk to more than one generation, our failure is due to the fact that we have never listened to more than one generation. Fathers need to listen to their sons. Mothers need to listen to their daughters.

Take into account the circumstances that surround boys and girls and young men and women. I am not patting you on the back. You are not angels, good or bad. You face temptations and too many of you do things that you should not do. I think youth lives as reasonably under all circumstances as ever before.

You say they live too rapidly. Of course they do. We all live too rapidly. Young people do not build the cars they ride in; they are seldom responsible for the environment in which they live; they do not write the books they read; they do not compose the songs they sing; they are not their own mothers, fathers, teachers and preachers! They receive these smack in the face.

I remember that when I was a boy in Lafayette, Oregon, we played baseball with a team in Amity, Oregon. It was ten miles away. When we started for our annual ball game we got up before dawn and milked the cows and were off in clouds of dust. No one knew if we had won or lost until we came home.

Now, when I travel from Lafayette to Amity, I cover those ten miles in a flash. Even the rooster lives faster than his ancestors if he gets across the road in time. We do live more rapidly now than we did twenty-five years ago if we survive.

I am bound to say this, young people, speaking directly to you, in these hurried times we have no chance of living the lives we would live, thinking our best thoughts and doing our best things without the strength and power and dynamic of Jesus Christ. Himself, who is the friend of youth—your friend and my friend.

I will tell you why Jesus Christ speaks to us, why He spoke to me in my youth and why He speaks to you boys and girls and young men and young women today. Jesus Christ speaks to all generations because He listened to all generations. He listened to the young and old, rich and poor; He listened to those who were in splendid shape physically and those in desperate condition physically, the hungry and blind. Because He listened to all these and found it in His heart to make response, He speaks to everyone in all circumstances now.

What about young people—good, bad, or indifferent? I will tell you this, men and women listening in, our sons and daughters, as I see it, are giving to us and to society greater return than we have any reasonable right to expect on the basis of time we have invested in them. The call is to us as well as to them, to set before them a good example and give them a good leadership, whatever their handicaps, to make their way toward a greater life.

Q   Do you think that young people are radicals? We hear so much of Communistic youth

A   Of course, there is always a danger here and everywhere. I think young people generally are more inclined to be conservative than radical Here again, those who speak and speak loudly misrepresent the rank and file. I like to think of young people as truly progressive. I do know young people; I have touched the lives of millions—directly. Always young people are loyal to fundamental democracy. In the United States the young people believe overwhelmingly in the Constitution of the United States and the Bill of Rights and all that they comprehend of civil liberties.

The meeting tonight, which is to place the emphasis on tolerance and true Americanism and on the spirit of youth in the United States of America, is characteristic of the youth of America and it is characteristic of Christian Endeavorers—hundreds of thousands of them—more than two million of them in the United States and the Dominion of Canada.

Q   The young people in our church are very much interested in our Christian Endeavor Society and work hard on their programs, but our pastor does not seem interested and does not cooperate. What do you suggest that we do about it?

A. It is hard for me to realize such a situation could exist. Scores and hundreds of pastors are at this convention. There is no excuse for a pastor's not being cooperative. I wish I could talk to this pastor. I wonder if the person asking this question would come and speak to me after this meeting. I would like to do something about it, and I can suggest what you can do about it.

I remember a pastor who came to a church in Columbus, Ohio, years ago. He was hesitant and he was afraid, and the Christian Endeavorers did something that warmed his heart and made him their understanding and generous companion. They invited him to come to their prayer meeting on the first Sunday evening after his arrival, and when he stood they showered him with roses from all sections of the Christian Endeavor room. Then they sang the song, "Is there anything we can do for you?" That pastor was ever afterwards their sympathetic friend. He is retired now, and when I saw him recently he told me of the lovely thing these young people did. So, if your pastor is not sympathetic, as you think, try something like that on him. Try roses on him. And give me his name and address.

Q. What church is the strongest in Christian Endeavor? Recently I was told that Christian Endeavor is a Presbyterian organization, but I know other denominations are represented in this convention.

A. You certainly know that other denominations are represented here. Of course Christian Endeavor is a Presbyterian organization; it is also a Baptist, Lutheran, Congregational, Episcopal, and United Brethren organization. Our societies are societies of the Baptist Temple in Philadelphia. My Christian Endeavorers are Baptists. Now in the United States the Presbyterian Church has more societies than any other church, although the Disciples of Christ are running them a close race. In Australia the Methodist Church has more than 90,000 of the 110,000 Christian Endeavorers of that country. The same is true in the Fiji Islands and New Zealand. So when you travel from place to place, from nation to nation, you find this church or that church predominating. But the unity is in Jesus Christ only. In South Africa the strength and numerical power of Christian Endeavor is almost exclusively in the Dutch Reformed Church.

Q. Has Christian Endeavor anything to say about the rising wave of intolerance in this country?

A. Christian Endeavor had something to say last night in regard to intolerance, and Christian Endeavor will have a great deal more to say tonight in regard to intolerance. Intolerance is the greatest social sin. That holds for individuals and it holds for races. You cannot keep another down without hurting yourself. We hurt ourselves, when we do that, more than we hurt others. Christian Endeavor, because Christian Endeavor tries to follow Jesus Christ, is against intolerance with all its might and all its power. We would not come into this city or any other city in convention if it were not possible for us to be entirely Christian in our program and in our hotels. In all our activities at home and abroad we recognize no line or race or color; we are one, and our unity is something dynamic in power.

Q. In your broadcast yesterday you said that denominational young people's societies and Christian Endeavor have the same principles. Why do they not get together?

A. I did say yesterday that the principles of the denominational groups— Epworth Leagues, B. Y. P. U.'s, Luther Leagues, etc., are the same, but organizationally we are not the same. I do think it is important that we should achieve a larger working unity, and it would interest you to know that the Trustees have authorized the President to send a communication to the youth leaders of all the churches, calling a conference for this fall of all youth leaders of all denominations, doing our level best to get closer to each other—to unite in doing those things that are our common heritage.

Q. Dr. Poling, are young women more religious than young men?

A. I do not think young women are more religious than young men. There might be more young women who are religious than young men, and I thank God that is true. But I find that some of the most dynamic Christian Endeavorers are young men. It is fortunate for us that so many young women are religious. It is fortunate for us that young men are being challenged to religious ideals and religious tasks. I find that young men and young women are incurably religious, and that represents the opportunity of the church. If all young people are incurably religious, what are we doing in the church and in Christian Endeavor to bring them into the life and fellowship of the church, in order that the Kingdom of God may be erected upon the earth? That is the question for us to answer.

Q. What is your opinion of the Bund? Should not all groups be allowed to carry on their programs under the free speech provision of the Constitution?

A I believe that all groups, of whatever character, should be allowed to carry on their programs under the Constitution, but not outside, not subversive, not contrary to the Constitution and the Bill of Rights. Whenever an organization or group—a Bund, Communistic group, or Fascist group—carries on a program alien to the very freedom that gives us the right of free speech, that organization, that program, should in the name of liberty, in the name of the Constitution, be investigated, and, if found subversive, should be closed up. I do not believe that any organization should be allowed to wear foreign uniforms or conduct a military program in the United States There should be for us one flag, one loyalty, always under God, and with first allegiance to Jesus Christ Himself.

Q. Are young people today interested in religion? I mean the overwhelming number of them Is it not a fact that church membership is falling off?

A That question is essentially the question that I have just answered. I have said that young people in a great body are incurably religious, and in this is the life of the church.

No, church membership is not falling off. Last year there was a net gain in the Christian churches of the United States of over one million. In many places there is a falling off in attendance at Sunday school and church, and to these lapses we must address ourselves.

XII

School of the Convention,

(Simultaneous Conferences)

THRONGS at the evening sessions, crowded streets alive with marchers and watchers as the parade goes by, a continent listening in as radio carries the messages of civic and religious leaders to American firesides! But without conferences, "the school of the convention," much of the spiritual and social benefit that will come from Cleveland 1939 could not have taken form and substance in human hearts.

Always the Christian cause has needed the definite, the specific, the organized way, to carry individual ideals and convictions into the common life of the day. It was so when Jesus dwelt among men: His disciples quietly, slowly, falteringly, learned His way and His purposes, and the church of Christ arose on those foundations, organizing truth for action. Christian Endeavor itself came into being with the evangelistic efforts that transformed men's lives, and by virtue of that, called for an educating of the willing mind to see human needs and, individually and collectively, to carry Christ's Gospel into dealing with those needs.

"Christ's Call," as heard by the throngs at Cleveland, was not solely a matter of great addresses, stirring music, and unforgettable worship services, important and inspiring as all these were. Deeply into the future the convention sped its way, by means of the leadership, group discussion, and influential Christian fellowship of its many conference sessions.

Conferences planned directly by the convention program committee occupied the time and attention of the delegates for more than two hours in each of four mornings. Friday, Saturday, Monday, and Tuesday mornings were quite largely devoted to this well organized, thoroughly planned "school of the convention."

More than one seasoned observer of this program was glad to acknowledge that these conferences, a regular feature of Christian Endeavor International Conventions, are unsurpassed throughout the whole denominational and interdenominational framework of American Protestantism. They are unique, not merely because Christian Endeavor plans them and provides them, but because the movement is in position to draw upon so wide and varied and able a list of leaders, because it gathers into this once-in-two-years congress of youth so completely representative and active a body of Christian youth, because the whole tone of the convention prepares for "greater things" in

93

conferences held at such a time and in such a setting, because the societies and unions of Christian Endeavor provide an effective and flexible and trusted mechanism for carrying conference ideals and decisions into definite action in the home communities across America.

The program of "Christ Calls!" was in the building for many months before the first sessions at Cleveland. Dr. Poling and members of the educational council dealt first with the basic concepts and objectives, and slowly the ideas began to take form in words and then in sentences. The Presidential address and the two-year program of objectives were simultaneously developed, each in harmony with the other. Two members of the educational council prepared the text of what became "The Program Guide," and then the other members of the council and the entire board of trustees of the International Society carefully weighed the suggestions and implications of this "guide" in terms of what all desired to see attempted and achieved by Christian Endeavorers from now until 1941.

Long before a conference leader at Cleveland faced his group, he acquired full information about the complete program of "Christ Calls!" and appraised its effect and significance in relation to the field of work with which his conference group would deal.

Conference Gleanings

What did the delegates have to say about the program of "Christ Calls!" as they faced its challenges in conference sessions day by day?

The mind of the convention is opened to us through the very complete file of reports, which substantially every conference through a duly appointed secretary has supplied to the International Society of Christian Endeavor.

Here are extracts from reports of the very first period of the Cleveland Convention conferences—occurring from 9:35 to 10:30 A.M. on Friday morning, July 7, when the theme was "Christ Calls to Christian *Endeavor*."

The Delegates Said·

"If we really endeavor we shall do more than just talk *Endeavor* suggests action. Let's do, not talk!"

"Be available for practical work. Our society (New York City) shingled the church steeple when there wasn't money on hand to pay workmen "

"We should carry church services to groups that are unable to attend. There are many people in old folks' homes, institutions, hospitals, jails, and ships to whom Christian Endeavorers can go and whom Christian Endeavorers will help."

"West Virginia Endeavorers held a two weeks' *youth* revival meeting "

"Services can be conducted in trailer camps and settlements of migrant workers. Sometimes our companionship in these places means almost as much as the religious service, for we shall try to bring our Christian Endeavor spirit with us into meeting these away-from-home transients in our community."

"Attract workers and employees to your meetings to discuss their problems. Be sure to consider the full implications of what it means to be a Christian in business."

Conference Plan

The general framework of the Cleveland Convention conferences was as follows:

The theme for each day, in the conference program, was chosen from the main divisions or headings of the "Christ Calls!" program— beginning, on Friday, with "Christ Calls to Christian *Endeavor.*"

In the first hour of conference sessions on each of the four mornings given to the convention's "school" eight groups of young people and four groups of High School Endeavorers met simultaneously to discuss the "Call" sounded in that theme, as applied to one's personal life, church life, and other relationship. Conference groups were made up on an alphabetical basis, and the leaders for various groups in the alphabet were assigned to these of course, quite at random. Delegates did not swarm into some room where a particularly popular leader would be heard, nor did all the Endeavorers from a given city or state come in a group into a single session among the dozen! "The magic of the alphabet" spread a delegation quite evenly through the whole range of simultaneous sessions—and quite obviously, no two leaders dealt in the same way with the subject and its possibilities, nor did any two conference groups arrive at identical results or conclusions.

A similar arrangement divided the Endeavorers for the second hour of conference sessions on Friday, the first, and Tuesday, the last, of the "school days." Better meetings and better organization were the subjects of simultaneous study.

For Saturday and Monday, in the second periods, a different plan was in use. Now were held simultaneous conferences that dealt with various specialized phases of Christian Endeavor and other church work and with special needs and interests within the personal living areas of young Christians. There were sixteen of these two-day conferences within the selection of the young people, eighteen and over, and ten others in the High School age group—which held its separate sessions in Cleveland College.

The conference schedule and leadership follows, in brief:

Friday, Saturday, Monday and Tuesday mornings—*Breakfa. conference* of all conference leaders and chairmen. Dr. J Gordon Howard, special chairman.

FIRST PERIOD CONFERENCES

Theme for Friday: "Christ Calls to Christian Endeavor."

Conference Leaders

Young People's Division (18 and over): Rev. Clifford Earle, Mr. J. W. Eichelberger, Dr. J. Arthur Heck, Dr. J. Gordon Howard, Rev. Herbert L. Minard, Mr. M. M. Shaw, Rev. Arthur Stanley, Rev. George Oliver Taylor.

High School Age Division (under 18): Dr. Paul C. Brown, Miss Lucy Eldredge, Mr. Warren G. Hoopes, Mr. Frederick L. Mintel.

Theme for Saturday: "Christ Calls to Christian Citizenship and World Peace."

Conference Leaders

Young People's Division (18 and over): Rev. Lawrence Bash, Rev. Ernest Bryan, Rev. Clifford Earle, Dr. J. Arthur Heck, Rev. Daniel K. Poling, Mr. M. M. Shaw, Rev. Arthur Stanley, Rev. George R. Sweet.

High School Age Division (under 18): Dr. Paul C. Brown, Miss Lucy Eldredge, Mr. Warren G. Hoopes, Dr. Raymond M. Veh.

Theme for Monday: "Christ Calls to Evangelism and Missions."

Conference Leaders

Young People's Division (18 and over): Rev. Lawrence Bash, Rev. Ernest Bryan, Miss Elizabeth Cooper, Rev. Clifford Earle, Mr. James W. Eichelberger, Rev. Daniel K. Poling, Rev. E. L. Reiner, Rev. Arthur J. Stanley.

High School Age Division (under 18): Dr. Paul C. Brown, Miss Lucy Eldredge, Mr. Warren G. Hoopes, Dr. Raymond M. Veh.

Theme for Tuesday: "Christ Calls to Personal Consecration."

Conference Leaders

Young People's Division (18 and over): Rev. Elmer Becker, Dr. Paul C. Brown, Rev. Clifford Earle, Dr. J. Gordon Howard, Rev. E. L. Reiner, Mr. M. M. Shaw, Rev. Arthur J. Stanley, Rev. George Oliver Taylor.

High School Age Division (under 18): Miss Lucy Eldredge, Miss Mary Jackson, Mr. Frederick L. Mintel, Mrs. Arthur J. Stanley.

SECOND PERIOD CONFERENCES

Theme for Friday: "Improving Our Christian Endeavor Meetings."

Conference Leaders

Young People's Division (18 and over): Rev. Elmer Becker, Rev. Clifford Earle, Glen Massman, John E. McCaw, Mrs. Luciel C. Nance, Rev. Chester Rutledge, M. M. Shaw, Rev. Arthur J. Stanley.

High School Age Division (under 18): Warren G. Hoopes, Miss Mary E. Jackson, Mrs. Arthur J. Stanley, Rev. George R. Sweet.

Saturday and Monday

There were sixteen different conferences in the Young People's Division (18 years of age and over) and ten different conferences in the High School Age Division (those under 18). These conferences covered a wide variety of subjects common to young people both in their personal living and in their Christian Endeavor connections. Practical methods were discussed.

Young People's Division

Preparation for Marriage. Consideration of the natural and basic forces at work in young people as they establish friendships and lay the foundations for years of happiness together. The Christian ideals and practices were pointed out and discussed.

> Leader: M. M. Shaw, Director of Young People's Work, United Presbyterian Church.

Worship in the Society. A study of the various elements which enter Christian worship as used in young people's societies, with recommendation of the best methods for development in worship.

> Leader: Dr. J. Gordon Howard, Director of Youth Education, Church of the United Brethren.

Training Christian Endeavor Officers. A study of the detailed duties of the officers of Christian Endeavor societies, the handicaps they need to overcome, the dangers they should avoid, and the methods to be used in developing leadership.

> Leader: Rev. George R. Sweet, Executive Secretary, Indiana Christian Endeavor Union.

How to Organize a Society. This conference sought to study and explain the steps to be taken in starting a Christian Endeavor society. Its material was valuable to pastors, directors of young people, and officers of Christian Endeavor unions.

> Leader: Glen Massman, Executive Secretary, Ohio Christian Endeavor Union.

What Are Christian Endeavor Essentials? A study of the basic purposes of Christian Endeavor; the application of important principles and the rejection of the unimportant. The distinctive features of Christian Endeavor received full attention.

> Leader: Frederick L. Mintel, Executive Secretary, New Jersey Christian Endeavor Union.

Christian Endeavor in the Total Program of the Church. The society's relationship to other interests and activities in the church. The important contributions of Christian Endeavor to a Christian program for young people

> Leader: Rev. Elmer Becker, General Secretary of Christian Education, Church of the United Brethren (Old Constitution).

Reaching Others for Christ. Personal methods of evangelism.

> Leader: Warren G. Hoopes, General Secretary, Pennsylvania Christian Endeavor Union.

Making the Most of Leisure Time. An appraisal of the uses to which leisure time may be put. What things are best? How may recreation become a constructive force? What new leisure-time pursuits are to be encouraged?

> Leader: Miss Elizabeth Cooper.

Getting Results from Publicity. Publicity methods and technique Best ways of advertising Christian Endeavor.

> Leader: Mrs. Luciel Nance, Executive Secretary, Kansas Christian Endeavor Union.

Missionary Action in the Society. A study of present-day missions, and things to be done by young people in behalf of missions.

Leader: Mrs. Helen Lyon Jones, Member of the Executive Committee of the International Society.

Chrstian Endeavor Covering Its Field. First period: What is the field of Christian Endeavor in the local church? What is its complete program? How may its full work be best accomplished? Second period: What is Christian Endeavor's field in the community? What young people should it reach? How may a Christian Endeavor union cover its full field of service?

Leader: Rev. Clifford Earle, Pastor, Lake View Presbyterian Church, Chicago.

Where Do I Belong in the World? A study of vocational choice and employment under present circumstances. How can a young person follow ideals in life-work?

Leader: George Oliver Taylor, Director of Young People's Work, Disciples of Christ.

Doing Something About Alcohol. Ways in which young people may meet the problems connected with drink. Study of youth action in community, state, and nation.

Leader: Rev. Lawrence Bash, Atlantic, Iowa.

The Devotional Life of the Individual. A study in personal development. The techniques of prayer, Bible study, meditation, reading, etc.

Leader: Rev. Daniel K. Poling, Pastor, Presbyterian Church, Bedford, New York.

Christian Endeavor for Adults. The upper side of graded Christian Endeavor. Adult societies. Alumni groups. The Sunday Evening Fellowship.

Leader: Dr. Paul C. Brown, Extension Secretary of the International Society.

Stewardship Is Essential! The full meaning of stewardship in the Christian life, and ways of success in practicing it.

Leader: Rev. Arthur J. Stanley, Associate President of the International Society.

High School Age Division (under 18)

All of these conferences were in Cleveland College.

The High School Society Counsellor. The adult counsellor of an adolescent group has many important functions. The qualifications, equipment and activities of this leader, together with his relationship to the society, were studied.

Leader: Miss Lucy Eldredge, Associate Director of Young People's Work, Congregational-Christian Churches.

Building a Program for the Society. A study of effective ways of charting the work of the society, organizing according to schedule, complete sharing of work, etc.

Leader: Rev. George Wilson, Field Secretary, Illinois Christian Endeavor Union.

Training Christian Endeavor Officers. A study of the effective development of society leaders. Applying Christian Endeavor details to human capacities.

Leaders: (Saturday) Dr. J. A. Heck, Director of Christian Education, The Evangelical Church; (Monday) P. Marion Simms, Jr., Field Secretary, New Mexico Christian Endeavor Union.

What Shall We Do in Leisure Time? A study of various hobbies and recreational pursuits. Good and bad ways of using free time.

Leader: John E. McCaw, Field Secretary, Iowa Christian Endeavor Union.

How to Make Missions Interesting. A study of modern and novel methods of missionary presentation and action. Missionary education in up-to-date phases. Leader: Mrs. Arthur J. Stanley, Fairport, New York.

Problems in Personal Conduct. A study of practical questions to be answered by teen-age boys and girls today, relating to school, home, friendships, amusements, etc. Leader: Ernest R. Bryan, Department of Education, Washington, D C.

How Can We Know God? How to develop a growing Christian experience
Leader: Rev. E. L. Reiner, Pastor, Waveland Ave Congregational Church, Chicago.

Reaching Others for Christ. How to make Christian personality winsome, and the Christian spirit contagious.
Leader: Rev. Leslie Deinstadt, Field Secretary, Massachusetts Christian Endeavor Union.

What Are Christian Endeavor Essentials? A study of the basic points in the Christian Endeavor Society.
Leader. Luther Medlin. Field Secretary, North Carolina Christian Endeavor Union.

Worship for Young Endeavorers. A study of worship plans and methods both for the individual and for the society.
Leader: Dr. Raymond M Veh. Editor, *The Evangelical Crusader.*

———o———o———o———o———

Theme for Tuesday: "Improving Our Organization."

Conference Leaders

Young People's Division (18 and over) Dr. Paul C Brown, Leslie G Deinstadt, Warren G Hoopes, Glen Massman, Frederick L Mintel, Arthur J Stanley, Rev. George R. Sweet, Rev. George H Wilson

High School Age Division (under 18) Miss Mary E Jackson, John E McCaw, Luther Medlin, Mrs. Arthur J Stanley

Special Conferences

Making a Success of Union Work. (Two periods a day, four days)
Leader: Ernest S. Marks, International Society of Christian Endeavor and Michigan Christian Endeavor Union.

Conference for Pastors and Directors of Young People's Work.
Leaders: (Friday) Dr. Daniel A. Poling; (Saturday) Harry N. Holmes; (Monday) Dr. William Hiram Foulkes; (Tuesday) Harry N. Holmes.

"The Fellowship of Prayer." (Four days.)
Leader: Mrs. Lillian D. Poling.

Denominational Conferences

Of great value and significance is the participation of national young people's leaders from denominational educational units, in the general conference program and in many other activities of the convention, including the meetings of the Board of Trustees.

The official leadership of a denomination again recognizes the importance of the convention experience and its relation to the future interests and work of young delegates, in the time and care given to denominational rallies and conferences, which have a definite and essential place in every International Convention program.

Among such conferences at Cleveland, held on Friday afternoon, were the following:

African Methodist Episcopal—African Methodist Episcopal Zion

Place: St. Paul's A.M.E. Zion Church.

Features: A joint program, with speakers and leaders from both churches, and with special musical numbers was presented.

Congregational-Christian

Place: Old Stone Presbyterian Church.

Features: In the general meeting—Speakers from the General Council, the State Council, and from local churches. At the dinner meeting—Miss Lucy Eldredge, Associate Director of Young People's Work, told about her recent tour of the world.

Disciples of Christ (Christian Church)

Place: Y.W.C A.

Features: Fellowship and discussion program with three discussion groups:

(1) "The Christian Youth Fellowship and Its Relation to Christian Endeavor " Leader, George Oliver Taylor

(2) "Materials for Use in Christian Endeavor."

(3) "Christian Endeavor in Action " Leader, W. Elbert Starn.

At the 5:30 banquet the toastmaster was Bob Fangmeier, of Highland Christian Church, Cleveland; song leader, W. Elbert Starn; speaker, George Oliver Taylor, National Director of Young People's Work.

Other features were provided by the Endeavorers of the Cleveland Christian Churches.

Evangelical

Place: Emanuel Evangelical Church.

Presiding: Dr. W. E. Peffley.

Features Charles Theuer, leader of singing; Harry Fussner, organist.

Special music provided by Evangelical Churches of Cleveland.

Period of Worship conducted by Rev. F. A Firestone.

Youth Address: Miss Esther Theuer.

Address "The Evangelical Church and Christian Endeavor," Dr. J. A. Heck.

Greetings from General Church Officers.

Supper, Dr. Raymond M. Veh, presiding. Singing and fellowship. Introduction of Evangelicals.

Presbyterian, U. S. A.

Place: Old Stone Presbyterian Church.

Time. 2:30 p.m. Leave for sightseeing tour of city.

4:00 p.m. Conference and rally.

6:00 p.m. Dinner and fellowship hour.

Features: The sightseeing trip included places of particular interest to Presbyterians. The rally presented many Presbyterian leaders. The dinner featured short addresses and a general social time.

United Brethren

Place: Mills Restaurant.

Chairman: Dr. E. E. Harris, Editor of *The Watchword,* Dayton, Ohio, active leader in state and county Christian Endeavor work.

Speaker: Rev. Harvey C. Hahn, President of Ohio Christian Endeavor Union; Director of Young People's Work, Miami Conference; Pastor, Otterbein Church, Dayton, gave the main address. Brief messages were given by Miss Claramae Wegner, chairman of arrangements for the rally, and Dr. J. Gordon Howard, General Director of Youth Education and Leadership Training, Dayton, Ohio. Pastors of Cleveland area were introduced. There was singing and a fellowship program, as well as a service of inspiration. Plans for "Youth Year" were announced.

United Presbyterian

Place: Russet Cafeteria.

Features: Guests and speakers: Mack Shaw, W Don McClure of Annuak Mission, and Al Heintz.

High School Conferences, Assembly and Banquet

Conferences for High School delegates were held in Cleveland College each morning. A general assembly followed the two conference periods each morning from Friday through Tuesday. The assembly program included a fellowship social sing, a brief address each morning followed by open forum, and a closing devotional service.

The Rev. Raymond M. Veh led the sing the first three mornings, and Miss Jean Fairfax of Cleveland on the last day. Dr. Veh spoke on Saturday and Monday and Miss Lucy M. Eldredge on Friday and Tuesday. The worship services were led by young people from Dayton the first morning, a group from the Evangelical Church of Cleveland on Saturday, delegates from Washington, D. C., and El Paso, Ill., on Monday, and by Miss Eldredge on Tuesday, when the assembly closed with a friendship circle.

Some questions presented in the question box and answered in forum period were these:

Do young people of China seem more or less sincere and interested in Christian Endeavor than American young people?

What shall a boy and girl do on a date?

What should I do when I have no money and the girls want to go out?

I have been going with a Catholic boy My parents are trying to break it up. What shall I do?

At our hotel some of the delegates took towels for souvenirs. Do you think that is right?

Last night I gave my life to Christ How am I to know what He wants me to do?

Is it showing disrespect to the church to have dancing in the church recreation room?

My parents do not approve of my friends. What should I do?

The High School (Intermediate) Banquet was held at the Euclid Avenue Baptist Church Monday evening. Albert Jones of Washington, D. C., was toast-master. Music was furnished by Miss Bohatic of Cleveland and Miss Elenor Chinnock of Canton. Short talks on "What This Convention Is Giving Me" were given by Charles Allen Jones of Pittsburgh, Florence Westman of Cleveland and James Duvall of Hamilton, Ohio. Mr. and Mrs. Bruce Dodd led the music period and Mr. Dodd led the group in the closing devotional moments. One hundred forty young people attended.

From Messages of Conference Leaders

To make Christian Endeavor devotional meetings effective: Maintain a high tone, spiritually speaking; this is a Christian *Endeavor* meeting. Be sure that time is given for prayer. Topics may include original subjects that suit the needs of the young people. Let the participants know in advance of the meeting what topic is to be considered; thus they will give it some thought. Employ variety: art and music, missionary programs of action, candlelight service, worship around a campfire, a broadcast meeting. Let the roll-call include a brief summary of your recent religious experiences and the forming of new convictions about Christ's Call.

—Elmer Becker.

Christian Endeavor is not merely a discussion club, but a group to go forward, advance, and do things—big things. Sit down with your fellow officers in the home church, with "The Program Guide" before you. Suggest the types of meetings that make for variety and information: the guest speaker (sermon), question-box, celebration of special days, meetings in which the whole society becomes the guest of some leader of thought and of action—all in addition to the more common and conventional type of meeting that does not always mean so much to some young people as it does to others.

—W. A. MacTaggart.

Perhaps twice a month it would be well to teach a new hymn to the Christian Endeavor society. More variety in the music will often help the meetings. We could read the song over together, before singing, so that we understand its message. Sometimes the emphasis is more certainly on learning the tune than on receiving the spiritual message that a great hymn imparts. The leader should be a person of enthusiasms, but also one who cares about promoting the Kingdom of God. He welds us together in a unique form of fellowship—the fellowship of worship in music. A call to worship should often take a musical form; perhaps a violin would lead.

—Luciel C. Nance.

In seeking to improve your society, why not give thought to these elements of the work, which are quite likely to require improvement? The devotional emphasis in the society's meetings. The matter of preparation for meetings, on the

leader's part and also on the part of the general membership. The type of leadership we provide for our meetings—a reflection of the spirit in which our meetings are conducted. Remember that Christian Endeavor rests on the idealism of youth. The society and its meetings have inspiration and power and challenge only so long as they lead on to Christ. We should not feel that we are trying too hard to get effective results, for are we not engaged in the biggest task in the world?
—*Warren G. Hoopes.*

The Christian Endeavor society should be more than "a meeting held once a week." Every member of the society deserves definite responsibilities, varied from time to time so that he gets a well-rounded training in Christian work. Just as the content matter of Christian Endeavor flows into committee work from the weekly meetings, so the organization strength of the society is developed through a sound, efficient executive committee. Here each committee is represented by its chairman, and here also are to be found all other officers of the society. The committee should meet once a month, preferably on a fixed date, and the members should feel their responsibility for being there. It is decidedly helpful to plan in this committee, and then publish for the whole society, a schedule for an entire year.
—*George R Sweet.*

Many churches seem to believe that Christian Endeavor activity ceases in the early twenties. Actually it does cease in many churches when boys and girls go off to college Yet colleges would do well to have Christian Endeavor societies on the campus instead of other types that somewhat break the ties young people have in the affairs of the home church. At college there can and should be a continuity between the work and objectives young people had in the home church and the type of work and purposes they will have on resuming fixed residence in some community and membership in its church, after graduation. All this points in the direction of adult Christian Endeavor societies, and definite provision and preparation for them Parents need this training and should set the example in Christian Endeavor membership to their children Special speakers should be the exception in the adult society's program. The best success is secured by making adult Christian Endeavor meetings expressional for everyone The adult society is especially useful when a merged or fellowship plan is used in the Sunday evening program of the church. (An explanation of the Saginaw plan for a complete Sunday evening Christian Endeavor program is given elsewhere in the Convention Report)
—*Paul C Brown.*

Christian Endeavor meetings are intended to encourage, inspire, and educate Let us picture the one who has come to your meeting for the first time Would he be encouraged to take part, to enter into public prayer, to seek closer acquaintance with the members—in short, to continue coming and sharing in such meetings? Suppose we study our meetings by the test: Is there anything in this meeting that will turn a visitor to accept Christ? What does this meeting of ours provide for the person who has come to it discouraged? All of these ends are served in the careful planning of our meetings and the selection and preparation of leaders We are bound to use each member in the leadership of our meetings, and there is much to be gained in matching the member to the topic he is to deal with. Advance choice of leaders not only prevents the mistakes due to haste but also gives a conscientious person plenty of time to do justice to the subject, by means of the reading, discussion, prayer, and even conference work in which he engages in the many weeks left open for preparation.
—*Chester R .tledge.*

Six essentials in fulfilling the purpose of Christian Endeavor:

1. Pledge. Some form of pledged obligation to be the basis for active membership.

2. Christian Endeavor meetings, held each week, to be well planned.

3. These meetings to be led by members of the society, with a reasonable number of variations and substitutions.

4. Definite forms of committee activity; the work to be well defined and widely distributed.

5. A yearly activities program, using "The Program Guide" as a means to suggest and assist with definite monthly emphases.

6. Union activities as a phase of every society's life. Send representatives to union meetings and activities. Let the society be well represented at very field event and at every conference.

—*Frederick L. Mintel.*

A special problem of Christian Endeavor societies is the possibility that cliques will be formed. There is such a tendency in some age groups and also in some communities. Suppose you provide something interesting and varied for each group, thus drawing all together through organized work and organized play. A clique can be separated by assigning people to widely scattered tasks and responsibilities within the church and society. Let all groups meet together for meetings that plan the society's program and objectives. The committee that develops into a clique may be urged to carry on some of its activities through sub-committee action. One group should not work together on the same tasks year after year. Vary the diet of each member.

—*Clifford Earle.*

Charter members of new Christian Endeavor societies are just about as important as were the charter members of the very first Christian Endeavor society. That is, they can and do have a great deal of influence, and hence we should help each society to start right. Suppose we consider the one feature of choosing proper leadership. You can nominate officers from the floor, which does away with charges of favoritism; yet sometimes the person who does the most talking and seems surest of himself gets the most votes. A nominating committee can confer carefully, consult the minister as to his preferences and observations, and talk with the person who is being borne in mind for each office in the society. Willingness to work counts for a lot—and the nominating committee has an opportunity to sense the individual's feeling about the office he might be chosen to fill. But the whole society can have a chance to nominate from the floor, so that the committee's slate is not shoved through without having the support of all the members behind it. It is well to do these things right. Persons should serve in an office as long as they are filling its duties and until a capable successor is ready. In making ready for a successor to a popular and efficient officer, remember that this gifted person was not always efficient and widely known; there has to be a beginning and we should help many to learn to lead.

—*Glen Massman.*

I suggest some immediate measures to meet the problems of alcohol. We should seek to build character strong enough to resist the temptation to drink. The nation requires a complete campaign of public education. Recreation of Christian Endeavorers and other groups should be studied and strengthened, so that it becomes more powerful as the obviously better way to enjoy good times. We should press local option wherever there is a way to advance this form of control. Elect dry candidates to office. Beer and dance halls should be separated. Advertising of alcoholic beverages should be seriously restricted, and eventually we shall want to prohibit all such. As long as men want to drink, they will be able to find drink in some form. The only permanent solution is that society and the church must provide an inner compulsion against drinking. We need to create more and more individuals who do not want to drink. and, of course, know that there is no good reason for wanting to drink.

—*Lawrence W Bash.*

Most of us need to create a better use of our leisure time. Make a chart of every quarter-hour for thirty days, and see how well satisfied you are with some of your uses of time. By all means, get over the habit of being late for appointments and duties. Use spare minutes in hobbies, handcraft, developing friendships, doing acts of kindness and engaging in service projects. Meditate, read the Bible, pray, in time that otherwise might be wasted. Our leisure time ought to be developing us; certainly it is a real test of the worth of our character and our purposes in life. Thus we shall develop certain abilities that otherwise would lie dormant. We shall add to our influence as active Christians in the community. We shall become a channel through which ideas and activities of value come into other lives.   —*Betty Cooper.*

In our trip around the world, we found Christian fellowship with many Christian Endeavor groups with whom we had no common bond in language. We could not fully understand what they tried to tell us, but we could see what in their Christian work and activities they were attempting to do for Christ and His church. In that was our fellowship; not in mere words. We were doing things together, and the barriers of language and nationality need not separate us. As Christians practicing a prayer life, it is often what we are trying to do rather than the words we use that determines the meaning of our worship to ourselves and to others.   —*Lillian D. Poling.*

The union constitution should be a live and vital instrument, guiding and controlling all union affairs. It should be a growing instrument, thus meeting new needs or changed conditions. Each union constitution should be revised, unless this has been done quite recently, so that it will be brought up to the present need. The constitution should cover purpose of the union, standards of membership, regulations, duties of department superintendents and of officers, a definite relationship with the world-wide movement and the International Society, which is the fellowship formed by all the unions of our continent. Have a constitution you can be proud of—and do not hide it away somewhere, until nobody knows where copies of it may be found and consulted!   —*Ernest S. Marks.*

A member of this conference describes as a common failure in Christian Endeavor work the fault of not developing the Lookout Committee to the extent of its possibilities and opportunities. Meet this situation by being certain that the membership of the society is classified according to active and associate members. Have a large enough and active enough Lookout Committee to keep closely in touch with the associate membership, making every appropriate effort to interest these young people in the Call of Christ for all of life and all of their loyalty. A three-three-three plan is sometimes employed. Suppose an active member (or an associate member) is not present for three consecutive Sundays. Three people send out cards reminding him that he is missed. Three people telephone him to express the same idea. Three others call on the absent member, expressing the hope that he can attend on the coming Sunday. Thus, nine people in one week's time have helped to make the one missing member feel that he is an asset to the organization and is bound to attend the meetings if he possibly can.

—*George H. Wilson.*

In our own United States, there are ten distinct groups that particularly need missionary help and action: Indians, Spanish Americans, Negroes, Japanese, Chinese, mountain people, migrants, miners, Alaskans, the West Indian people. So important are these needs that Christian Endeavor societies are strongly urged to conduct weekly mission study classes at certain seasons, not depending solely on a few Sundays each year for the missionary work emphasis. There is much value in so utilizing the missions idea that those about us, realizing how strongly we feel about bringing others to know Christ, will feel constrained to know Him better and associate themselves more fully with Christian work.

—*Helen Lyon Jones.*

Among what young people shall we recruit for Christ? Where are we going to get to know those who should be coming to Him? We shall know of some through school friends, of others through neighbors with whom we talk about our Christian interests. You can have cards printed to pass out to children on street corners, inviting them to a church meeting and to the Sunday school and Junior society. Be certain to ask to the church and school and Christian Endeavor society persons who are not as financially well off as we are; make them feel that they are really welcome. Canvass the entire community on occasion to find new prospects. And bring those from your own home into a close, personal fellowship with Jesus Christ.   —*Leslie G. Deinstadt.*

Am I sociable? Can I find and make friends—one of the finest of Christian accomplishments? These are some tests: A sociable person enjoys being with people He does not easily get his feelings hurt. He enjoys people more than he does things He never deliberately avoids meeting some other person. He welcomes and aids those who come for advice; indeed, you can test your attractiveness to others by noticing how many people want to get counsel from you. When discouraged, the sociable person seeks company instead of trying to hide himself and store up his discouragements. Try to determine the things that interest you most, and find friends who have the same interests. But then determine what things in addition you should be interested in, and by your friendships find your way into those areas of living.   —*Moses M. Shaw.*

Among High School Conferences

To make missionary meetings more interesting: missionary museum; collecting things from foreign countries; visit schools and other spots that have such collections from abroad; missionary reading, missionary correspondence; use of missionary slides and movies; some magazines especially feature missionary work or the people with whom such work is done.   —*Mrs. Arthur J. Stanley.*

The certain and final goal of leadership is that one's work and influence shall not be bounded by narrow dimensions and one special kind of work. We shall try to develop leadership ability in all ways. We should try to determine where we need more help and experience to become useful to the church and society, and look for more knowledge and practice there, instead of solely in the types of work we are sure to do well.   —*J. A. Heck.*

A Christian Endeavor society should keep going all the year around. We cannot give over the summer to the reign of evil and indifference. Not only the summer months are lost, but many weeks in the fall show poor results, if we "go on vacation" in Christian Endeavor work. Good fellowship is necessary to a society, but all laughing and talking and evidences of disrespect should stop when a meeting begins. The pre-prayer service not only greatly helps and strengthens the leader and others participating, but should begin the Christian Endeavor sessions in the Christian spirit.

—Mary E. Jackson

How to measure a meeting: Was the room in which it was held attractive? Were the chairs, hymnals and Bibles neatly in place? Did the service begin on time? Were the leaders well prepared? Were hymns carefully chosen? Was there a spirit of reverence? Did all who attended participate? Was the Scripture well and reverently read? Were the prayers meaningful and effective? Did the service make a real contribution to the lives of those who attended?

—Raymond M. Veh

Christian Endeavor societies can work for world peace—by helping young people to become intelligent about world problems; by meeting with facts the misrepresentations sometimes given by newspapers, radio, and newsreels; by publishing a Christian citizenship bulletin in which goodwill is served by appreciative items about other peoples and races. Peace plays will help. The society should make its influence felt on members of Congress, when measures affecting peace and international relations are under discussion

—Lucy Eldredge

Note the difference between idle time and leisure time! Idle time can become dangerous, but leisure time is invested in well-being. Religious institutions are therefore wisely interested in leisure time, that it may be spiritualized. Here we have freedom to choose, such as we may not have as to school and work time and assignments. In leisure time, let us cultivate friendships, secure physical exercise, develop cultural interests and appreciation of the fine arts, learn skills.

—John E. McCaw

XIII

"We Here Highly Resolve . . ."

IF evidence were needed to show the utter seriousness of the Cleveland Convention delegates, their realistic approach to current problems, their determination to take immediate Christian action toward the solution of those problems, such evidence abounds in the resolutions passed by the convention. These resolutions emphasize the importance of Christian attitudes and of prayer, they insist upon the expression of those attitudes in action.

They who were not present at the convention but who do read this report are urged to give very serious consideration to the resolutions and to cooperate with the delegates in the action which the resolutions suggest.

World Peace

When the peace of the world hangs precariously by only a thread, as it does today, wishful thinking is not enough. Christian Endeavor stands for Christian action on behalf of peace. We would be realistic as we look out upon a world beset by distrust, fears, and bitter animosities. We recognize that the causes are deeply rooted and that they can no longer be ignored. We are conscious of the fact that no one easy, simple solution will solve the problem. We, therefore, as Christian Endeavorers representing the two million youth of the North American continent who are affiliated with our great movement for Christ and the church, do hereby—

1 Affirm anew to all the world at our convention that only by peaceful means can the economic, cultural, and political problems of our hard-pressed world be solved in a permanent, satisfactory manner.

2. Resolve that isolation is no solution for world peace as far as America is concerned. We cannot solve problems by ignoring them, wishing that they did not exist, or by trying to stay away and isolate ourselves from them. We are a part of the world; the problems of the rest of the world are, of necessity, our problems, and we must strive for their solution.

3 Resolve that the only sure way of keeping America out of a world war is to make sure that there is no world war. If we would keep America out of war, we must strive for world peace by adjusting the causes of friction. We must assume leadership in movements and conferences to adjust these differences and difficulties out of which the seeds of war are fast springing even as we meet here tonight.

The world has sacrificed much—far beyond its means—for war. It must be willing to sacrifice in economic resources, in trade advantages, in territorial claims, yes, even in pride and prestige, for the sake of peace.

4. Resolve that men of good will must arise in every nation to see to it that this is done. To that end we extend our Christian greetings and pledge our good will to the peoples of all nations. We recognize the "oneness" of humanity under God and pray to Him that all of His people may dwell together peaceably on the face of the earth.

Stop Sale of War Materials and Munitions to Japan

This convention having listened afresh to the horror of the undeclared war now devastating China in violation of sacred and solemn treaty obligations and recalling how China implicitly trusted the collective security that guaranteed her sovereign integrity, confesses its humiliation and shame when it remembers that the majority of the raw materials used by the invading armies comes from the United States.

We feel the agony of this participation and call upon our government to prohibit the export of war materials and munitions and other essentials for the waging of war.

We cannot feel that international friendship is well served by helping an aggressor nation conquer a practically defenseless people, bringing suffering to them that baffles adequate description.

Our attitude is one of absolute friendship to the people of Japan, whose Christian leader, Kagawa, is one of the noblest spirits of our time and with whom we feel the closest spiritual kinship.

Civil Liberties and Tolerance

The International Christian Endeavor Convention, whose membership is so largely drawn from the United States and the Dominion of Canada, pledges anew its devotion to the principle of religious and civil liberty.

It believes in the American way of life—of the people, by the people, and for the people.

It stoutly stands for freedom in thought, freedom in public worship, and freedom in public assemblage

It places itself squarely against all the "isms" that threaten to undermine democracy, whether Fascism, Nazism, or Communism

It deplores every form of intolerance and bigotry, whether religious or racial, and it especially deplores and disavows anti-Semitism as a flagrant violation of fundamental human rights and of contradiction of the mission and message of Christianity.

Traffic and Commerce in Beverage Alcohol

WHEREAS, total abstinence was the stand of Christian Endeavor as organized in 1881; and, WHEREAS, the slogan, "A saloonless nation by 1920" was the rallying call that came out of the Atlantic City International Convention in 1911; and, WHEREAS, we believe that the Eighteenth Amendment and national prohibition were a direct result of a unity in the field of temperance action that began with Christian youth; and, WHEREAS, we realize that now after six years of repeal, our nation faces a problem in the liquor traffic which is more intense and terrifying than the problem of thirty years ago—

We, the Christian Endeavorers of the United States and Canada, assembled in 37th Convention, go on record as being unequivocally opposed to the traffic and commerce in beverage alcohol.

We condemn all forms of liquor advertising and the widespread use of billboards along our highways as a medium of liquor advertising; also advertisements in magazines, newspapers, and over the radio We do commend, moreover, those newspapers that refuse to sell space for liquor advertising and the radio stations that will not sell time to commercial agencies advertising the sale of beverage alcohol.

We are convinced that one of the best methods of meeting the challenge of repeal is through temperance education, and do most aggressively encourage all forms of temperance education which show the very definitely harmful results of alcohol.

"Christ Calls!" and as youth answering that call, we recommend that a definite program of action be followed by the International Society of Christian Endeavor in cooperation with other Christian agencies now at work.

We accept the challenge of repeal and, spurred by it, work to the end that the liquor business goes

—off the air
—out of print
—off our billboards
—out of human lives
                                          —through enlightened youth.

Gratitude for Cleveland's Hospitality

The 37th International Christian Endeavor Convention hereby places on record its profound sense of gratitude to Cleveland for the warmth and open-hearted generosity of its hospitality and the amazing efficiency of the convention management. Words are a feeble instrument to express our affectionate thoughts of this great city set by the blue inland sea—our gracious host for an unforgettable week. We believe Cleveland helped us to write religious history. We believe Cleveland has enabled a new note of faith and hope to go echoing up and down the pathway of our land. As we return home we shall carry enshrined in our hearts the spiritual and moral heights we found in the throbbing center of your great city.

The enumeration of all the persons and organizations that have shared in this youth enterprise would be well-nigh impossible, but especially we would salute in this tribute the following:

The Cleveland committee of arrangements, its officers and the membership of all its committees,—a noble body of devoted men and women under the leadership of a very prince of chairmen and one of the great Christian laymen of our land, Fred W. Ramsey.

The mayor of the city for his welcome and his constant presence and who with other city officials cooperated in all possible ways.

The police for constant, kindly and effective courtesy.

The management and personnel of the Public Auditorium for every thoughtful consideration.

Hon Herbert C. Hoover, and the Governors of New York and Ohio, who by prophetic utterances from our platform gave it national and international distinction

The churches, the ministers, who with hundreds from their congregations, gave active support.

The American Legion, its officers and members who marshalled the parade, the memory of whose witness will linger through the years.

The staff of the Y.W.C.A., the Girl Reserves, and the Christian Endeavor groups for ushering at the meetings. We felt guided to our seats amid a pageant of loveliness

Never has a convention received more generous recognition by the Press of a city. *The Plain Dealer*, *The Cleveland Press* and *The Cleveland News* in their editorials, pictures and featured articles have interpreted the inward spirit of the convention with rare understanding.

The radio stations and broadcasting companies for large gifts of valuable time. making possible vast unseen audiences.

The merchants and advertising companies for much friendly help and publicity.

The large, loyal and glorious choir for a ministry of music under magnetic leadership and the services of Vincent H. Percy at the great organ.

The Statler Hotel for generous gratuitous provision of Convention Headquarters for five months.

Cleveland College, its officers and trustees for accommodation for conferences

Old Stone Church. its pastor and trustees for rooms for the Junior Convention.

Euclid Avenue Baptist Church, its pastor and trustees for cooperation in the organization and training of the choir.

The Cleveland Convention Board for invaluable assistance in promotion and arrangement.

The officials and members of our Christian Endeavor Unions in Ohio for friendship and open-hearted kindness.

The General Assembly of the Presbyterian Church for the loan of a communion service of over two thousand pieces.

The speakers and conference leaders whose notable contributions have enriched every hour. We would forget no one.

You have made possible a memorable experience. enriching heart and mind. and hosts of young people will live brighter, happier, and more useful lives because of Cleveland 1939.

We heard the call to Cleveland and at Cleveland heard the call of Christ, and from Cleveland we go to translate its message into action.

Cleveland. we thank you!

Christian Endeavor's Sixtieth Anniversary

The 37th International Christian Endeavor Convention rejoices with thankful and grateful hearts in anticipation of the celebration in February. 1941. of the sixtieth anniversary of the founding of Christian Endeavor Dr and Mrs Francis E. Clark initiated and inspired a movement that has girdled the world with a golden ministry of youthful service for Christ and the Church We desire that the Executive Committee plan some adequate and worthy recognition of the sixtieth anniversary of world-wide Christian Endeavor expressive of our thanksgiving to God for long years of blessing and service.

Thankfulness for President Poling's Leadership

The 37th International Christian Endeavor Convention, meeting in Cleveland. Ohio. places on record its profound thankfulness to God for the continuance during the years of the inspiring and prophetic leadership of its honored and beloved President. Dr. Daniel A Poling.

We especially respond to his great message given to us at this convention with its wide horizons, its challenge for Christian witness and action, and its call to individual, social, and national redemption in the power of the living Christ

We have felt the inescapable truth that "Christ Calls!" above every clamoring voice of man and pledge to our President. with joyous acclaim. our faith in him and our loyal cooperation with heart, mind, and hand to translate his program into the life of our society, our country, and the world.

World Conference of Christian Youth

We, the Christian Endeavor delegates of the 37th International Christian Endeavor Convention, meeting in Cleveland, Ohio, U. S. A., send our greetings to the World Conference of Christian Youth.

We feel that you will make history in this conference as you plan for the program of the Christian youth of the world. May the plans that are made at this conference help all Christian youth in establishing world peace and world brotherhood and aid in bringing church unity and world-wide evangelism.

We anticipate using the report of this great conference of world Christian youth.

Our greetings are being sent to the conference by Dr. Stanley B. Vandersall, the Secretary of the World's Christian Endeavor Union, and the youth delegates of Christian Endeavor attending the conference.

We will remember the conference in our prayers, for we feel that our convention at Cleveland has led us to answering the call of Jesus Christ in action and service for His cause.

The National Christian Mission

The 37th International Christian Endeavor Convention records its warm and hearty approval of the National Christian Mission to be held in the United States and Canada in 1940-1941 under the auspices of the Federal Council of Churches. We note with real satisfaction that the President, two of the Vice-Presidents, and several trustees of our organization are members of the national committee. Christian Endeavor in furnishing some of the leaders is thus intimately associated with this great cooperative evangelical thrust of the Protestant churches. We are also proud of our part in the remarkable Universities' Christian Mission which visited the campuses of twenty-five universities, welcomed by students and faculty.

Christian Endeavor has a special sense of kinship with such throbbing spiritual enterprises, so evangelical in purpose, and evangelistic in objective. We call upon Christian Endeavorers in all the cities to be visited to give active cooperation and support to the Mission, and thus to assist in making a vital and nation-wide spiritual achievement with world-wide influence.

XIV

The Junior Department of the Convention

THE two hundred and fifty Junior boys and girls who gathered for their banquet on Thursday noon in the Parish House of Old Stone Presbyterian Church were the first testimony to the genius for leadership of Mrs. Cecil A. Berry, chairman of the Cleveland Junior Committee. Appointed early in April, Mrs. Berry found no Junior leadership in Cuyahoga County Christian Endeavor Union, and but one Junior Christian Endeavor society—in Calvary Reformed Church, which has sponsored Junior Christian Endeavor for forty-seven consecutive years. She recruited her committee and, with their help, enlisted the enthusiastic cooperation of Junior churches, mission bands, Junior choirs, and Junior church school departments in the banquet and in the more largely attended Junior session of the convention on Thursday afternoon.

The various church groups at the banquet were introduced by Mrs. Berry and welcomed by Richard F. Denham of the First Presbyterian Church in East Cleveland. The Old Stone Junior Church is much interested in puppetry and, under the direction of Mrs. Hugh H. Kissane, shared an Old Testament story with an appreciative audience.

The instrumental music for the Junior session was furnished by Mrs. Rita George True, Windermere Methodist Church, organist, and Mrs. Richard Gilpin, Highland Christian Church, violinist.

The programs for the session had been bound in covers bearing Hofmann's "Boy Christ" in color, so that each Junior could frame the picture for his own prayer corner at home.

"Joyful, Joyful, We Adore Thee" was used as a processional for the combined Junior choirs from Brooklyn Memorial Methodist, Calvary Evangelical, Euclid Avenue Baptist, Fourth Reformed, Hough Evangelical, Old Stone Presbyterian, Ebenezer Evangelical, Cleveland Christian Home, Highland Christian and Windermere Methodist Churches.

Under the direction of Mrs. Herman Klahr of Old Stone Presbyterian Church, the choirs rendered "Fairest Lord Jesus" responsively, with Franklin Kissane reciting the Scripture.

Miss Wilma Thompson, Ohio Junior Superintendent, who presided with Mrs. Berry, introduced the speakers, Dr. Daniel A. Poling, President of the World's Christian Endeavor Union, Dr. Stanley B. Vandersall, Associate Secretary of the International Society of Christian Endeavor, and Fred W. Ramsey, chairman of the Cleveland Convention Committee, who gave to the boys and girls the feeling that they were really part of the larger convention.

The hymn, "We Would See Jesus," was used in preparation for the presentation of Elizabeth Edland's dramatization, "Children of Galilee," by Juniors from the Highland Christian and Lakewood Congregational Churches under the direction of Mrs. J. W. Fulton and Mrs. Joseph Rinehart. The children of Galilee knew and loved Jesus before His crucifixion. Rejoicing in His resurrection, they learn how many there are who want to see Him, and decide they have much to do as His followers.

Progressing steadily toward the climax, the program closed with the worship service, and the children's answer to Cnrist's Call in the spoken words of the hymn, "Dear Lord, We Give Our Youth to Thee." This service was conducted by Miss Viola Oltman, Minneapolis, Minn.

The headquarters for the Junior program was in Old Stone Presbyterian Church in the Public Square. The church and all its staff were most generous in making available the church's many facilities. The Junior service room was really five connecting rooms, and the Cleveland Junior committee had arranged them to meet the requirements of the program. The Cleveland Public Library through Miss Edna Hull had sent cases and several hundreds of selected books. There were pictures, posters, and a variety of exhibits shared by Junior groups. A multitude of resource materials had been assembled, and two hours were definitely set for "discovering" them.

Opportunities for friendly fellowship were the distinguishing mark of this convention. This gracious atmosphere was created by the members of the Junior committee, who greeted all who came to the service room, registered them and badged them with little blue and white Junior C. E. shields on silk cords. The warm cordiality of Wilma Thompson, the state hostess, and the assistance of especially appointed hostesses from among the state superintendents cultivated every opportunity.

The Round Tables

A wonderfully fine group of state Junior superintendents or their official representatives from nineteen states and one Canadian province met in seminar the first hour each morning. Using a check list assembled from their own questions, they indicated the order of subjects for consideration, which centered in the effective functioning of the state organization, the training of leaders, the building of state programs, the preparation of bulletins, the choice of topics and the provision of topic helps, and the make-up of the state Junior superintendent's portfolio. Sub-committees in the fields of program and topics cooperated most helpfully. The earnest request of the state superintendents is for more time in conference at International Conventions.

To each member of this group is due grateful acknowledgment for their generous and whole-hearted cooperation at every point of the program. On Friday evening, they gathered for dinner with Dr. and Mrs. Poling and Dr. Vandersall.

Conferences for Junior Workers

The Junior workers in the second-hour conferences each morning enjoyed the help of Miss Viola Oltman, Minneapolis, Minn., who is experienced in the work with Junior boys and girls in Junior Christian Endeavor, Sunday church school, and vacation and weekday church schools.

Miss Oltman had written a new unit in the field of Junior worship, "Thinking About God.' The Junior society of Calvary Reformed Church under the leadership of Mrs. Florence Handy and Mrs. Hazelle M. Moore had used the first two sessions of this unit, "God the Creator," and "God Our Father," and were ready to follow the guidance of Miss Oltman in the last two topics, "God Our Helper" and "A Service of Meditation and Worship." This demonstration was not intended as an ideal program, but rather as a part of a typical ongoing piece of work suitable for the devotional meetings of any Junior Christian Endeavor society. The first hour together on Friday was given in part to preparation for observing the demonstration.

The new Christian Endeavor Program of Activities for the biennium, 1939-1941, centered in the theme, "Christ Calls!" was presented by Dr. Stanley B. Vandersall, Associate Secretary of the International Society of Christian Endeavor. It was the unanimous request of the state superintendents that an adaptation of this program be made available to the workers with Juniors.

On Saturday, the Juniors from Calvary Reformed Church came bringing collections of stones, leaves, and pictures, which they had begun as they talked of "God, the Creator." Upon their arrival, they found a browsing-table with articles and books which would interest them. When all were present, they were called to the piano to learn a new song which later was to be used in the worship service. They then went to the discussion circle where they talked over their ideas of God. They discovered that people of long ago knew God as a Helper. Many of them were named and their stories found in the Bible. The fact that God helps us today, but that we must do our share in striving for the right was the climax of the discussion. There being a feeling of worship in the room, the pianist stepped to the piano and played softly while the children took their places in the worship corner.

The girls and boys took charge of the service, with Miss Oltman telling the story. There was a deep feeling of reverence shown by the children.

The Juniors reassembled on Monday morning for the last session of "Thinking About God," which was a "Service of Meditation and Worship." Before going to the worship center the group discussed the meaning of worship. Prayer and the realization of God's presence through meditation and quietness were stressed. A litany of praise was worked out by the group. When all were ready for worship, they went to the worship corner for the service, led and conducted by the Juniors. The service consisted of quiet music, the call to worship, the Scripture, the litany of praise, the Junior leader's presentation, the hymn, "For the Beauty of the Earth" (two verses), the poem. "God Is Near," prayer, the hymn, "How ·Strong and Sweet," the story, "Pippa Passes," and an appropriate verse in benediction.

The Junior workers on Tuesday morning discussed and evaluated the materials and methods used in the demonstration hours of Saturday and Monday, and Miss Oltman answered the questions which had arisen.

Miss M. Virginia Hopkins, Maryland Junior Superintendent. brought greetings from the Junior workers in the World's Christian Endeavor Convention at Melbourne, Australia, which she attended last year.

The Parents' Hour

On Sunday afternoon came the Parents' Hour in Old Stone Church, with Dr. Poling presiding. (See Chapter VII.)

During the Parents' Hour, provision was made for the children in the chapel. A chalk talk was given by J. W. Everhard. The boys and girls enjoyed a story by Mrs. Carl R. Brown, and were led in singing by Mr. Rodeheaver.

The Vesper Service of Dedication

The generous hospitality of the Cleveland Junior Committee found a delightful expression in the courtesy tea extended to all Junior workers at the close of the Parents' Hour. Mrs. Arline Jordan at the piano and Mrs. Richard Gilpin on the violin played a program of sacred music during the tea and in the vesper service.

From the restfulness of this informal hour, the Junior workers entered into their candlelight service of dedication. The service had been sent to Mother Clark and to all state superintendents that they might keep the hour with us, wherever they were. Many messages were received in response.

Beneath a large and beautiful copy in color of the picture "Follow Me," by Tom Curr, which hung against a blue background, stood an altar with a rustic cross, on which candles had been placed. Answering Christ's Call to "let your light so shine," the state superintendents lighted their candles from the cross, returned to their places at the front of the room and passed the light back from row to row. Upon the challenge, "Go Shine for Me," they formed a processional from the service room. From this service they went to the Auditorium, where Dr. Poling presented each state superintendent and representative to the convention.

Fellowship Luncheon

Another fellowship occasion was the World Friendship Luncheon on Monday noon in the dining room of Old Stone Church. World Tour tickets had been sold, twelve of which were punched for each of the ten tables representing one of the countries where missionary work is being done, and each "traveler" started out with a little silk American flag.

The travel department of Higbee's store in Cleveland cooperated by furnishing a large ship model, a lighted globe, and colorful travel posters for background. The flags of the nations were loaned by the Rotary Convention. The luncheon chairman, Mrs. Ruth Warren, is the recreational director of an international settlement, and had access to many lovely and authentic pieces for the tables. Some beautiful decorations were brought by Mrs. William V. Martin of Illinois, who, with Mr. Martin and Miss Florence Vander Molen of Michigan, helped Mrs. Warren to arrange the tables. Borrowing from the crowded curio cabinets of Old Stone Church, from Mrs. Walvoord, returned Japanese missionary, from Mrs. McLean in Colombia, and from Mrs. John Henry Mastin returned from Chile, and from world travelers, the tables were intensely interesting.

There was a hostess at each table from the Junior committee. Mrs. C. A. Berry presided and presented the members of her committee. Mrs. William E. Bowyer, Secretary, Mrs. Fred Faile, Mrs. Christian. Mrs. W. E. Juergens, the three of whom served also on the Junior Committee in 1927, Mrs. Hugh Kissane, Mrs. Wayne Handy, Mrs. Ruth Warren, Mrs. J. W. Fulton, Mrs. Emmit Ong, Mrs. Harry Smoyer, Mrs. Wilbert Warnicke, Mrs. A. Otto Reiser, Mrs. Joseph Rinehart. The introductions were acknowledged and sincere and grateful appreciation was expressed to Mrs. Berry and the committee members on behalf of the International Society and the luncheon guests. Mrs. Harry Smoyer gave an appropriate solo.

The guest speaker most fittingly was Miss Lucy M. Eldredge of Dayton, O., Associate Secretary of the Young People's Department of the Congregational and Christian Education Society. The young people of her communion had sent her on a world tour, from which she had just returned, and she very realistically shared with her listeners some of the high spots of her experience.

With illustrations from the trip Miss Eldredge emphasized the following points:

1. It is very natural for children to be interested in children and life in other lands, and so we have a keen interest upon which to build our world friendship activities.

2. Friendship grows as we discover we have things in common with other people. We are alike in so many fundamental ways, that likenesses rather than differences which make other people seem queer should have main emphasis.

3. World Friendship is an indispensable part of our program because so many people in all parts of the world need our friendship.

4. World Friendship is an indispensable part of our program because only through wide interests and friendly sharing can our boys and girls grow as Christian persons.

Grateful acknowledgment is made to the officers of the International Society of Christian Endeavor, to Mr. and Mrs. William V. Martin, and to the very considerable number of individuals and agencies whose generous and helpful cooperation made possible this Junior program.

The Ohio State Convention

The 54th Annual Convention of the Ohio Christian Endeavor Union was held in conjunction with the 37th International Convention, under the leadership of State Executive Secretary Glen Massman and State President Harvey C. Hahn, both of Dayton, O.

All the inspirational sessions of the International Convention were those of the Ohio Convention which had several unique features of its own. At 5:45 Saturday afternoon the Administrative Committee met at the Statler Hotel. On Saturday night, following the evening session at the Public Auditorium, hundreds of Ohio's delegates went to the main Ballroom of the Statler Hotel for what was known as "Ohio's First Foodless Banquet." Arthur F Briese, noted Chicago lecturer, was the principal speaker. Other speakers were Mr. Massman and Rev. Harvey C. Hahn.

On Monday the Board of Trustees of the Ohio Union met with the Ohio delegates in the annual business session.

Each evening the Ohio delegation had an assembly for a devotional service in Room C of South Hall. Miss Geneva Craig, International Prayer Meeting Superintendent, led these devotional services. The closing meeting was held Tuesday night, with a message brought by the State President. Following this meeting a group of Ohio delegates left for a conducted tour of the New York World's Fair.

XV

In the Exhibition Hall

D ELEGATES arriving early for general sessions—and it was amazing
how many of them came ahead of time—found one section of
Convention Hall a never-ceasing source of interest. This was the
Exhibit Hall, in which there was so much to awaken interest and
suggest new activities for Christian Endeavor societies.

Starting at the right of the entrance door your attention was held at
once by the exhibit arranged by the American Mission to Lepers. Here
George C. Southwell, first Christian Endeavor Life Work Recruit, Mrs.
Southwell, and their committee answered the countless questions of
delegates who paused to admire the replica of the Endeavor Village,
built in Luebo, Belgian Congo, by contributions of many Christian
Endeavorers and crowned by the Poling-Massman Church. Only $18
will build a little house for a leper or leper family, and many delegates
determined to start a project for raising that much money as soon as
they returned to their societies. A good way to begin to raise the
money, some of them decided, would be to hold a special meeting and
show the moving picture, "Song after Sorrow," obtainable without
charge from the American Mission to Lepers, 156 Fifth Avenue, New
York, N. Y.

Other Endeavorers bought pig banks in which to save a personal
contribution for the missionary work among lepers.

You wanted to linger a long while in the booth housing the exhibi-
tion of the World's Christian Endeavor Union. Here was so much to
admire. An exquisitely embroidered white silk map showed the position
of Christian Endeavor in China, red circles with the C. E. monogram
in white indicated places where communication with other parts of
China and the outside world is as usual. Yellow circles indicated places
where communication is difficult, gray circles indicated Christian Endeavor locations in the war zone.

The number of societies in each center was shown by numerals under
the circle. You grew dizzy trying to count up the total and were forced
to buttonhole Dr. Vandersall and ask, "How many C. E societies are
there in China?" and rejoice at his answer.

An unusually lovely embroidered silken banner was the gift to
Dr. Francis E. Clark of Dr. W. S. Ament, hero of the Boxer Rebellion.
It was made by the girls in the Congregational Girls' School in old
Peking, and its symbolism was as striking as its colors were harmonious.
The Church of China was represented by lotus flowers coming up
through the muddy waters, signifying affliction. The Chinese sign

for fire, around the edge of the banner, also told of persecution. The C. E. monogram held the names of Endeavorers who were martyred, the men's names being embroidered in the C, the women's in the E.

South India was represented by a collection of coins given by the natives of Tirimangalam for the Christian Endeavor Museum in Boston.

Korea had sent a white silk banner with embroidered letters in red.

Christian Endeavor publications in many languages lay open upon the table. You noted the *Quarterly Bulletin* of South Africa, the *Victorian Christian Endeavor News* of Melbourne, Australia, and the *South Australian Christian Endeavor News.* You glanced at *Die Kristelike Strewer—Konferencie Nommer* from South Africa, *Jugendsieg* from Poland, and *Entschiedenes Christentum* from Germany.

Near a picture of Williston Congregational Church, Portland, Me., in which Christian Endeavor began, hung a copy, in Dr. Clark's own handwriting, of the original constitution of the first Christian Endeavor society. Here indeed was the beginning of the great world movement of which you are a part. You turned from it to look with grateful eyes at the pictures of Dr. and Mrs. Francis E. Clark, the founders, Dr. and Mrs. Daniel A. Poling, the present well-loved leaders, and the Rev. and Mrs. Vere Abbey, who direct the Christian Endeavor work in India, Burma and Ceylon.

In the Indiana booth Miss Maxine Mendel showed you photographs of Christian Endeavor activities, including local society groups, delegates to the summer retreat at Bethany and to the Kansas City and San Francisco Conventions, and Kansas Endeavorers on post-convention tours. A very beautiful state banner was examined with much interest.

In the Pennsylvania booth, attention was attracted by a curious Christian Endeavor quilt. Made of patchwork, each patch bore the autograph of a prominent Christian Endeavorer. The names of Mother Clark, the Polings, the Abbeys of India, appeared. Many names represented Endeavorers in other lands—India, England, Japan, the Irish Free State, Canada, Mexico, China, Hawaii, and the Philippines were noted. Mrs. William Ensminger of Marysville, Pa., was the proud owner of this amazing quilt. She had done the embroidering, and ten friends, working fifty hours, had done the quilting in the form of C. E. monograms.

The program materials for all branches of Christian Endeavor work in Pennsylvania for 1939-1940 were displayed on very well-designed posters. You stopped to examine many of them, observing that they included Evangelism, Society and Union Guidance, Publicity, and Research, Missionary, Floating Welfare, *Youth Today* (the state Christian Endeavor magazine), *The Christian Endeavor World*, Recreation, Quiet Hour, Union Planning, Adult Work, and Finance. Truly a most imposing evidence of well-planned Christian Endeavor work. In the Canadian booth Mrs. George McQueen and Stanley Patterson were glad to answer questions regarding the progress of Christian Endeavor in Canada. Posters showed beautiful views of Ottawa, Toronto, and Montreal, and illustrated folders of Canada were pleasant souvenirs for United States delegates. Mr. Patterson had also some lovely pictures of King George and Queen Elizabeth, taken during their recent visit to Canada.

The Presbyterian Church in the U. S. A. had its booth well filled with posters showing helpful materials for young people's work.

Adjoining it the Golden Rule Union of Washington, D. C., was bright with golden banners and copies of the "Golden Rule" printed on tiny rulers.

Bright cut-out posters of unusual attractiveness were displayed by the Congregational Union of Cleveland. They showed the contrast between Prejudice and Inter-racial Fellowship, War and Peace, Gangs, and the Creative Use of Leisure. Here also was a copy of the Statement of Purpose of the Pilgrim Fellowship.

The Virginia Union's exhibit included scrapbooks of unusually original Christian Endeavor posters and wall posters of burnt wood.

The Michigan Union's display of posters of helpful materials was exceptionally interesting. The poster showing "How Records of All Societies Are Kept" was greatly admired. The practical uses of the mimeograph were illustrated by posters and bulletins and the advertising possibilities of photographs were shown by pictures of the Grand Rapids Convention.

Even more interesting were the striking photographs of the Detroit Christian Endeavor Union at work. Here you could see Endeavorers visiting the Children's Hospital, conducting Christian Endeavor services for boys and girls in the Detention Home, and making committee visitations to prospective members.

Posters on Christian citizenship and a poster map of the Michigan Christian Endeavor unions also appeared. An especially well designed poster showed Michigan's work against liquor advertising and for the control of liquor traffic.

The United Brethren Church's booth challenged, by means of posters, the adults to take an interest in young people's work. Young people were urged to apply Christian principles in choosing a vocation and to work for peace and against intemperance.

Bob Brown and Dorothy Sprietsma, in the Illinois Christian Endeavor Union booth, proudly showed the state paper, *The Endeavorer*, and county union papers, Peoria's *The Gleam*, and the *Winnebago County News*. Posters advertised the state convention and photographs showed the 3,814 members of one of the state's largest Sunday schools —that of the Third Presbyterian Church of Springfield.

The program materials and activities of the Y.P.C.U. were on display in the United Presbyterian Church's booth.   Posters, news bulletins. pictures, impressive banners told the story.

Nearby, the booth of the Disciples of Christ overflowed with informative leaflets, generously given away and an extensive presentation of materials useful in carrying out the youth program.

Miss Ruth Hoon, presiding at the booth of the Disciples of Christ, showed an exceptionally attractive and complete display of mission study materials for young people and materials for every phase of local church young people's work.   Pictures of summer conferences, mounted on posters, made you want to register for at least one conference immediately.

A thoughtful tour of the Exhibit Hall was bound to give the delegates new ideas and new incentive to make the work of their own Christian Endeavor society more successful.

As always the International Society of Christian Endeavor offered unlimited helps to effective work in the Convention bookstore in the lobby.   Here a courteous corps of salespeople worked under the direction of Mrs. Leila Heath Neff, and gave invaluable aid to inquiring Endeavorers.

"CHRIST CALLS!"

A Program of Activities

for

Christian Endeavor Societies and Unions

1939—1941

Adopted by the Board of Trustees of the
INTERNATIONAL SOCIETY OF CHRISTIAN ENDEAVOR
and released at the biennial
International Convention at Cleveland, Ohio
July 6-11, 1939

I. Christ Calls to Personal Christian Experience and Growth.

A. Every active Endeavorer definitely acknowledging his open commitment to Jesus Christ as Saviour and Lord.

> Strive continually to maintain personal Christian experience as the basis for membership in the society
>
> Reach young people who are not Christians with a view to winning them to the acceptance of Jesus Christ and His way of life

B. Every active Endeavorer striving for personal growth in Christian living.

> Make a habit of Bible study.
>
> Read the best religious literature
>
> Establish private devotional practices
>
> Participate frequently in public worship
>
> Cultivate Christian friendships.
>
> Lay the foundations for happy and successful home life.
>
> Recognize always the supreme authority of Christ in all matters of personal and social conduct

C. Encourage the personal growth of all members in the society.

> Enroll every reachable person as a Comrade of the Quiet Hour.
>
> Promote regular attendance at the worship services of the church.
>
> Enlist Endeavorers and other Christians as tithers, and enroll them as members of the Tenth Legion.

123

Set every Endeavorer actively at work in the society and church, each having one or more specific tasks and responsibilities.

Give frequent opportunity to young people to speak in testimony of their Christian experience.

Encourage all members to influence others to commit their lives to Christ, using such means as
> prayer groups,
> personal workers' bands,
> pre-Easter meetings,
> decision services,
> pastors' study classes.

Promote participation in active enterprises of the Kingdom.

D. Use the Christian Endeavor covenant as a basis of membership, relating the individual to Christ, to the organized group, and indirectly, to the larger program for young people in the church and in the world.

E. Establish some plan of personal counseling on the problems of young people, such as:

(1) choosing vocations in terms of first and second preferences, (2) finding Christian values in one's work, (3) using recreation as a means of character growth.

> Use pastoral interviews,
> question-and-answer periods,
> guided discussion,
> and other methods

II. Christ Calls to Church Loyalty and Fellowship.

A. Encourage young people to be loyal, thorough, and effective, in church membership, church attendance, church financial support.

B. Enrich public and private worship by study and adaptation of methods and elements of worship.

> (Examples, art, hymns, prayers, responses, symbols, improved meeting place.)

C. Share actively in the total educational program of the church, through

> Representation of each society in the church's committee on young people's work (or Christian education);
>
> Leadership training classes and courses;
>
> Graded Christian Endeavor (one society, or more, for each definite age group);
>
> An adult counselor for each High School and Young People's society;

Cooperation with church school activities, as in recruiting youth for teaching and leading classes.

D. Dedicate individuals and the group to definite forward steps in helping the church to grow and to discharge its responsibilities.

(Examples: evangelistic campaign sponsored or aided; united Christian program in the community promoted; youth enrolled in definite training program for society and church leadership.)

E. Emphasize through study and example the principle that every Christian is a steward of his time, talents, money, and life, all of which belong to God.

III. Christ Calls to Christian Action in the Community.

A. Unite with other Christian forces to evangelize the community.

(Examples: community vacation Bible schools; visits to homes in a given area; reaching newcomers as they enter the community; public meetings; cooperation with local missions.)

B. Promote and improve local cooperation and unity among Christian groups.

Support the local union of Christian Endeavor

Encourage fellowship with other youth groups, interdenominational activities, missionary groups, peace groups, good citizenship and temperance groups, etc., which have kindred ideals and purposes in the development of a Christian community.

C. Sponsor and conduct recreational programs that will improve the use of leisure time.

Christian Endeavor recreational events bettered, given more variety, and opened on occasion to larger numbers of the youth of the community.

Cooperate with other agencies (such as schools and colleges, Christian associations, Allied Youth, and athletic leagues) to raise the standards for youth's good times.

Locate specialists in the various constructive hobbies and cultural interests, helping young people to know these men and women and to learn new skills and interests from them.

D. Join with other constructive forces for civic betterment.

Promote law observance and enforcement.

Remedy prejudice and injustice.

Protect Sunday, the Lord's Day, from commercialism and irreligious uses.

Deal with the issues of gambling, unwholesome moving pictures, harmful reading-matter, habit-forming drugs, the use of alcohol, and any other forces detrimental to the Christian development of youth.

Strengthen organizations and programs which aid inter-racial goodwill and the preservation of minority rights.

E. Seek facts and form Christian attitudes on economic justice and the protection of producers, workers and consumers.

Study and utilize the principle of cooperatives, including credit unions.

Interest labor union groups, employers, and the churches in knowing and understanding one another.

By study groups, demonstrations, and exhibits aid Christian youth to become intelligently Christian in the use of buying power, personal budgeting, and contributions to religion and social service.

IV. Christ Calls to Christian Citizenship in Nation and World.

A. Support Christian missions around the world. . . for Christ calls all men unto Him.

Promote missions by prayer, special meetings, circulation and study of mission books and magazines, drama, films, and guest speakers.

Contribute to denominational and interdenominational missionary activities, the latter to include the influential work of the World's Christian Endeavor Union in mission lands.

B. Bring together Christian youth around the world in fellowship and understanding.

Study the history and culture of other peoples and their contributions to mankind.

Read, circulate, and discuss books and pamphlets on peace and ways to attain it.

Participate in international travel and in widely representative gatherings, such as the International and World's Christian Endeavor Conventions.

C. Promote the World Peace Fellowship of Christian Endeavor, and other steps toward peace.

The World Peace Fellowship is an enrollment of Christian Endeavorers and all friends of peace for the study of and concerted action on current strategic points in the cause of peace. Its *faith* is that mankind is one great brotherhood, indivisible alike by social position, religion, nationality or color, God being Father of all. Its *aim* is to destroy those barriers which separate man from man, to substitute for them a Christian comradeship, and to foster "the spirit that does away with the occasion of wars." It seeks to unite believers in peace in fellowship and devotion to an ideal rather than to singleness of method in attaining it.

D. **Attack national and world problems of maladjustment, suffering, and oppression.**

Know the facts behind narrow prejudices that affect minority races and groups.

Encourage friendly relations with other races.

Study the causes of crime, and arrive at ideals and practices that seek to offset these causes and to set high examples.

Strengthen goodwill among Catholics, Jews, and Protestants.

E. **Educate concerning the harmful effects of alcohol and other narcotics, including tobacco, with particular reference to effects wrought among adolescent boys and among girls and women.**

Campaign against advertising for liquor and cigarettes, in whatever medium used: magazine, billboards, newspapers, moving pictures, radio.

Inform the public of alcohol's menaces to public health and to public safety (as in automobile accidents).

Plan education against narcotics, utilizing meetings, addresses, books, charts, laboratory demonstrations, quiz programs, radio presentations, etc.

Support local, and larger, campaigns for strict regulation of the liquor trade, including restriction of hours of sale, looking toward elimination of the sale of alcoholic beverages.

www.ingramcontent.com/pod-product-compliance
Lightning Source LLC
Chambersburg PA
CBHW020041040426
42331CB00030B/119